Integrating Higher Education Planning and Assessment: A Practical Guide

by

David Hollowell

Michael Middaugh

Elizabeth Sibolski

Society for College and University Planning
339 E. Liberty Street, Suite 300
Ann Arbor, Michigan 48104
Phone: 734.998.7832
Fax: 734.998.6532
Web: www.scup.org

ISBN 0-9700413-9-X

Table of Contents

Foreword

By

George Keller

There is no shortage of books about planning, nor of guides to its practice at colleges and universities. But this terse book is uncommon.

For one, it has a lucid prose style and glides along on greased paragraphs. The writers are also exceptionally clear about what they regard as central, and what colleges need to pay attention to above all. The text is full of wise suggestions and mercifully silent about novel gimmicks. The chapters exude the authors' years of experience and the sound judgment they have gained.

Yet, given the recent and swelling demands for better accountability for results of the nation's huge investment in higher education, this book neatly fuses educational planning with assessment of the plan's success or shortcomings. Assessment is a precarious field, an adolescent enterprise, still plagued with nebulous recommendations and demands. This book sheds as much light on assessment as seems possible, and offers useful ideas and tools for everyone in higher education or in policymaking.

Advice and wisdom are usually not offered together. In this book the two cavort.

Preface

Various types of planning take place at most colleges and universities—academic planning, enrollment planning, human resources planning, budget planning, facilities planning, campus master planning, and so on. The concern in the early 21st century ought not to be whether planning is occurring in higher education, but how effective that planning is. All too often, planning is compartmentalized into categories such as those just delineated, without focus on the quality or the interconnection and integration of planning. Whether developing a master plan for campus design for the next twenty years, planning for the implementation of a new academic discipline within the next five years, or planning how to address an unanticipated shortfall in revenues that have, in fact, been already spent, certain consistent threads run through good planning processes and practices.

In this volume, we focus on the generic structure of planning and argue that planning falls into three basic categories: academic planning, human/fiscal resources planning, and physical resources planning. *It is our position that academic planning is the engine that drives all other types of planning at an institution.* Our task is to illustrate this concept, and we do so through a series of examples from institutions across the United States.

We also underscore that planning is more than setting goals and objectives. *Good planning must include sustained analysis and assessment of progress toward goals and objectives.* Good planning must also include a component directed at communication. Diverse audiences exist within virtually any planning activity, and it is important to communicate directly and effectively with each of those constituencies.

As noted previously, this volume is about the appropriate uses and integration of planning and assessment throughout the fabric of an institution. It should not be viewed as, nor is it intended to be a definitive text on, any specific type of planning and/or assessment. Readers who are searching for how-to guides in areas such as academic planning, student learning outcomes assessment, and campus master planning should consult the many other excellent sources available on these subjects. This volume will be much more helpful to those who are seeking ways to better understand and integrate the planning and assessment activities that go on in many places and at different organizational levels of an institution of higher education.

A number of different audiences may find the information in this volume helpful. Presidents and chief academic officers may use the ideas in this book when thinking about and managing planning and assessment processes. Faculty, staff, and others charged with implementing planning and assessment processes (at institutional or unit levels) may find concepts, examples, and suggested resources particularly useful. In addition, those who are charged with institutional accreditation responsibilities should find that development of linked planning and assessment processes provides a meaningful way to demonstrate to external reviewers that the institution is really doing what it says that it is.

It is important that we acknowledge and explain briefly our decision to offer extensive examples from the University of Delaware. Two of the authors have guided the planning process at this institution for more than a decade. This intimate familiarity with the nuances of how planning and assessment have developed on this campus allows for the presentation of a case study that is rich in detail. In effect, we are able to provide an insider's view of planning and assessment at an institution where these functions have been highly valued over a significant period. It would not be possible to provide the same level of detail if examples were limited to an outsider's description of the planning and assessment processes at other institutions. In addition to significant

case material from the University of Delaware, we refer to multiple examples of best practices at other two- and four-year institutions.

It is also important to note that the examples presented in this volume are from institutions located in the United States. However, we believe that the concepts presented are useful to institutions wherever they are located.

We also caution that this volume is not intended as a treatise on the theoretical underpinnings of good planning. Our central focus is on the provision of useful advice and guidance. However, we do offer a significant amount of contextual information and an extensive bibliography for those interested in more theoretical approaches.

This book is about effective planning in colleges and universities. It is intended as a practical volume that explains why planning is important and describes the various types of planning and the integration of planning into the fabric of institutional processes, the various audiences within and external to the institution that play important roles in planning, and the expected outcomes from good planning. It is not a cookbook, with replicable recipes for planning processes. Rather, it is a tool kit with basic planning concepts that can be adapted to the specific needs of the diverse spectrum of institutions that constitute American higher education in the early 21st century. We believe that you'll find it valuable.

Chapter 1

Introduction

We take it for granted that the exponential growth in American higher education since the end of World War II is the product of careful academic and institutional planning. At the close of the war, the GI Bill flooded campuses with a tidal wave of ex-soldiers seeking baccalaureate degrees and bringing with them federal funds that signaled a new prosperity for colleges and universities, particularly in the public sector. Later, the 1960s saw massive infusions of federal funds on college campuses, and the 1970s witnessed the arrival on campuses of the baby boomers, with unprecedented pools of tuition dollars.

When enrollments declined in the 1980s as the baby boomers graduated, colleges and universities were fiscally stressed. That stress was compounded by economic downturns in the early and late 1980s. When the economy began to recover in the mid-1990s, colleges and universities discovered that they were no longer unquestioned favorites when it came to governmental funding or private and foundation giving, having been replaced by K–12 education, health care, and public safety. As tuitions escalated, parents and legislators questioned the value of the return on tuition investment, asking what students really learned.

Although not new to the higher education community, the call for accountability has gained strength in recent years, particularly as it concerns student learning outcomes and the efficient use of human and fiscal resources. The escalating emphasis on accountability is related, in part, to perceptions that colleges and universities do not plan carefully or assess their effectiveness. Indeed, the Council of Regional Accrediting Commissions, which comprises representatives from the major regional accrediting bodies throughout the United States, anticipates that a major component of legislation to renew the Higher Education Act currently under consideration in Congress will be a call for greater public accountability with respect to student learning, transparency in reporting and disclosure, assurance of the quality of distance learning, and assurance of the ability to appropriately transfer credit.

Institutions clearly must plan, and understand the extent to which those plans are successful, if they are to remain vital, vibrant, and viable. The importance of planning and assessment to institutional vitality is underscored by the emphasis on these criteria for regional accreditation throughout the United States. The approaches to and emphasis on planning and assessment are not uniform among the regional accrediting agencies, but it is important to note the similarities. Examples taken from the current accreditation standards or criteria of the regional agencies illustrate these similarities.

The **Middle States Commission on Higher Education** has four accreditation standards that are directly related to planning and assessment:

Standard 2: Planning, Resource Allocation, and Institutional Renewal

An institution conducts ongoing planning and resource allocation based on its mission and goals, develops objectives to achieve them, and utilizes the results of its assessment activities for institutional renewal. Implementation and subsequent evaluation of the success of the strategic plan and resource allocation support the development and change necessary to improve and to maintain institutional quality.

Standard 3: Institutional Resources

The human, financial, technical, physical facilities, and other resources necessary to achieve an institution's mission and goals are available and accessible. In the context of the institution's mission, the effective and efficient uses of the institution's resources are analyzed as part of ongoing outcomes assessment…

Standard 7: Institutional Assessment

The institution has developed and implemented an assessment process that evaluates its overall effectiveness in achieving its mission and goals and its compliance with accreditation standards…

Standard 14: Assessment of Student Learning

Assessment of student learning demonstrates that, at graduation, or other appropriate points, the institution's students have knowledge, skills, and competencies consistent with institutional and appropriate higher education goals. [1]

The **Commission on Institutions of Higher Education, New England Association of Schools and Colleges**, includes the following requirements for institutional accreditation:

Standard Two
Planning and Evaluation.

The institution undertakes planning and evaluation appropriate to its needs to accomplish and improve the achievement of its mission and purposes. It identifies its planning and evaluation priorities and pursues them effectively.[2]

The **Higher Learning Commission's Criteria for Accreditation** include two that are specifically relevant to the topics addressed in this volume:

Criterion Two: Preparing for the Future.

The organization's allocation of resources and its processes for evaluation and planning demonstrate its capacity to

1. Middle States Commission on Higher Education, *Characteristics of Excellence in Higher Education: Eligibility Requirements and Standards for Accreditation* (Philadelphia: Middle States Commission on Higher Education, 2006), ix–xi.

2. Commission on Institutions of Higher Education, *Standards for Accreditation* (Bedford, MA: Commission on Institutions of Higher Education, 2005), 4.

fulfill its mission, improve the quality of its education, and respond to future challenges and opportunities.

Criterion Three: Student Learning and Effective Teaching.

The organization provides evidence of student learning and teaching effectiveness that demonstrates it is fulfilling its educational mission.[3]

The **Northwest Commission on Colleges and Universities** includes among its standards for accreditation the following:

Standard 1.B—Planning and Effectiveness.

The institution engages in ongoing planning to achieve its mission and goals. It also evaluates how well, and in what ways, it is accomplishing its mission and goals and uses the results for broadbased, continuous planning and evaluation. Through its planning process, the institution asks questions, seeks answers, analyzes itself, and revises its goals, policies, procedures, and resource allocation.

Standard 2.B—Educational Program Planning and Assessment.

Educational program planning is based on regular and continuous assessment of programs in light of the needs of the disciplines, the fields or occupations for which programs prepare students, and

other constituencies of the institution. [4]

The **Commission on Colleges of the Southern Association of Colleges and Schools** includes the following among its comprehensive standards:

3.3 Institutional Effectiveness.

3.3.1 The institution identifies expected outcomes for its educational programs and its administrative and educational support services; assesses whether it achieves these outcomes; and provides evidence of improvement based on analysis of those results. [5]

Two of the accreditation standards of the **Accrediting Commission for Senior Colleges and Universities of the Western Association of Schools and Colleges** (WASC) are particularly relevant to this discussion:

Standard 2
Achieving Educational Objectives Through Core Functions.

The institution achieves its institutional purposes and attains its educational objectives through the core functions of teaching and learning, scholarship and creative activity, and support for student learning. It demonstrates that these core functions are performed effectively and that they support one another in the institution's efforts to attain educational effectiveness.

---

3. The Higher Learning Commission, *The Handbook of Accreditation*, version 1:10/03 (Chicago: The Higher Learning Commission, 2003), 3.2-5 and 3.2-8.

4. Northwest Commission on Colleges and Universities, "Accreditation Standards," Redmond, WA, www.nwccu.org.

5. Commission on Colleges, Southern Association of Colleges and Schools, *Principles of Accreditation: Foundations for Quality Enhancement* (Decatur, GA: Commission on Colleges, Southern Association of Colleges and Schools, 2001), 22.

Standard 4
Creating an Organization Committed to Learning and Improvement.

The institution conducts sustained, evidence-based, and participatory discussions about how effectively it is accomplishing its purposes and achieving its educational objectives. These activities inform both institutional planning and systematic evaluations of educational effectiveness. The results of institutional inquiry, research, and data collection are used to establish priorities at different levels of the institution, and to revise institutional purposes, structures, and approaches to teaching, learning, and scholarly work.[6]

Finally, the **Accrediting Commission for Community and Junior Colleges of the WASC** includes the following among its standards for accreditation:

Standard I: Institutional Mission and Effectiveness.

The institution demonstrates strong commitment to a mission that emphasizes achievement of student learning and to communicating the mission internally and externally. The institution uses analyses of quantitative and qualitative data and analysis in an ongoing and systematic cycle of evaluation, integrated planning, implementation, and re-evaluation to verify and improve the effectiveness by which the mission is accomplished.[7]

The central threads running through all of these accreditation requirements is that planning is essential and must be systematic, rooted in an institution's mission, predicated on analytical and evaluative information, and used for institutional decisions, especially resource allocation. Let us be clear: imperatives of accreditation aside, institutions must plan effectively to be effective. Where that is the case, the accreditation process becomes, in part, an affirmation of the evidence of that effectiveness.

6. Accrediting Commission for Senior Colleges and Universities, Western Association of Schools and Colleges, Handbook of Accreditation (Alameda, CA: Western Association of Schools and Colleges, 2001), 20 and 29.

7. Accrediting Commission for Community and Junior Colleges, Western Association of Schools and Colleges, "Introduction to the Accreditation Standards," Novato, CA, www.accjc.org.

Chapter 2

Structuring the Planning Process

In thinking about what goes into a good planning process, a useful starting point is to consider what planning is not. In his classic 1983 volume, *Academic Strategy: The Management Revolution in American Higher Education*, George Keller listed 10 things that strategic planning is not:

1. It is not the production of a blueprint…

2. It is not a set of platitudes…

3. It is not the personal vision of the president or board of trustees…

 4. It is not a collection of departmental plans, compiled and edited…

5. Strategic decision making is not done by planners…

6. It is not a substitution of numbers for important intangibles…

7. It is not a form of surrender to market conditions and trends…

8. Strategic planning is not something done on an annual retreat…

9. It is not a way of eliminating risks…

10. It is not an attempt to read tea leaves and outwit the future…[8]

The cautions Keller offered more than twenty years ago continue to represent vital concerns that may imperil good planning today. We return to each caution briefly, offering some thoughts about why each is important today.

1. *The production of a blueprint.* While planning goals and objectives should be documented—indeed, most academic accrediting bodies require it—that planning document is not an immutable course of actions. Internal and external contexts and situations change, and flexibility is required so the plan can respond to reality.

2. *A set of platitudes.* It is fine for an institution to aspire to provide the finest undergraduate education in the nation or to promise that no academically qualified student will be denied admission because of inability to pay for a college education. It is encouraging when an institution promises competitive compensation for all employees or state-of-the-art research facilities for its faculty. However, these are not plans; they are aspirations that require careful charting of measurable action steps that lead to implementation. It is the identification of a course of action that transforms aspirations into reality through planning.

8. George Keller, *Academic Strategy: the Management Revolution in American Higher Education* (Baltimore: Johns Hopkins University Press, 1983), 140–42.

3. *The personal vision of a president or board of trustees.* Like it or not, good planning is broadly participatory, embracing active input from the major constituencies that make up a college or university as well as the major constituencies that the institution serves. A president or board may want an institution to be transformed into a major research university, while the fiscal base at the institution, as well as the regional economy, may be best suited to provision of solid undergraduate education consistent with the workforce needs of local employers. Without dialogue between and among the institutional leadership and those that they serve, meaningful planning is not possible. While these conversations, at times, can be both controversial and contentious, they are essential to successful planning activity.

4. *A collection of departmental plans, compiled and edited.* All too often, particularly at smaller institutions without institutional research and planning offices, institutional planning is a bottom-up activity. That is, organizational units plan for their respective needs, and the output from those units' plans are in some way collated and edited into a college-wide "plan." However, to ensure institutional progress and improvement, there has to be a true institution vision and sense of direction in planning, with planning at the unit level tied clearly and specifically to that institutional vision and direction.

5. *Done by planners.* Large, complex higher education institutions frequently have planning offices with staffs of varying size. While an institution may have an office of facilities planning, for example, the specifications for what goes into a new classroom building or student center had best come from outside that office. Similarly, if an institution has an associate provost for academic planning, he or she should coordinate curriculum planning among the faculty, rather than impose a preordained directive for curriculum development. As noted previously, good planning is broadly participatory.

6. *A substitution of numbers for important intangibles.* A strong institutional research and analysis capability is an essential component of good planning. However, any institutional researcher worth his or her salt will quickly point out that in any analysis, it is possible to find relationships and estimates that are statistically significant but not important, while it is also possible to find relationships and estimates that are important, but not statistically significant. It is the interpretation of information and numbers, based upon experience and familiarity with the planning context, that supports good

decision making.

7. *A form of surrender to market conditions and trends.* While planning must be sensitive to environmental contexts, it must remain true to institutional mission. In the late 1970s and early 1980s, as schools competed for students, a number of traditional liberal arts institutions created and staffed departments catering to majors in business and computer science, where employment market demand was heavy. However, as these programs burgeoned nationally, the job market eventually became sated, and some institutions were left with fully tenured departments and undersubscribed enrollments. While institutions do need to be nimble in today's environment, nimbleness should not be at the expense of the institution's core mission.

8. *Something done on an annual retreat.* Planning is an ongoing, iterative process. It is not done in August and reevaluated the following August. Planning goals and objectives should be analyzed and evaluated throughout the year. As goals are achieved or become outdated or obsolete, they should be replaced with appropriately current goals and objectives. Good planning processes are characterized by rolling, cyclic activity and regular institutional research to determine progress and/or the need for change.

9. *A way of eliminating risks.* While good planning should minimize

institutional vulnerability, it is not characterized by an absence of risk taking. For example, Wells College, a small liberal arts college on the shore of Cayuga Lake in upstate New York, was established in 1868 as a college for women and remained a single sex institution until recently. As is the case with many small, tuition-dependent institutions, the need to expand enrollment forced Wells College to reexamine its mission and admit men beginning with the fall 2005 freshman cohort. Such a decision is not without substantial risks, including alienation of a portion of alumnae donors, the absence of any historical information on the proportion of male students offered admission that will ultimately decide to attend, and the need to redefine student services to be consistent with and appropriate within the context of coeducation. If the decision results in a substantial growth in enrollment, and concomitant tuition revenue, the decision will appear sage. As planning initiatives of this sort are implemented, institutions need to evaluate them constantly to determine if the risk was worth the effort. (It is worth noting here that a significant number of institutions have faced this specific problem in recent years.)

10. *An attempt to read tea leaves and outwit the future.* Good planning relies on empirical forecasts and projections. But those forecasts and projections should be targeted to

specific goals and objectives. If an institution decides to increase the size of its undergraduate student body, that decision should, in part, be predicated on forecasts that suggest that the college-bound pool of high school graduates likely to select the institution will be sufficient to support that decision. But the policy must also be rooted in an institution-wide belief and commitment that it is the right thing to do at this point in time, given the institution's instructional, academic support, and student services capacity.

In his classic volume, Keller also delineates six characteristics of good academic and strategic planning. These characteristics emphasize and summarize many of the points noted above. However, where Keller describes characteristics of effective academic and strategic planning, we suggest that those characteristics are actually consistent throughout all types of good planning.

1. Academic strategic decision making means that a college, school, or university and its leaders are active rather than passive about their position in history…

2. Strategic planning looks outward and is focused on keeping the institution in step with the changing environment…

3. Academic strategy making is competitive, recognizing that higher education is subject to economic market conditions and to increasingly strong competition…

4. Strategic planning concentrates on decisions, not on documented plans, analyses, forecasts, and goals…

5. Strategy making is a blend of rational and economic analysis, political maneuvering, and psychological interplay. It is therefore participatory and highly tolerant of controversy…

6. Strategic planning concentrates on the fate of the institution above everything else.[9]

Figure 2.1: A Categorical Taxonomy of Higher Education Planning

Academic Planning	Resource Planning	Facilities Planning
Instructional Curriculum	Human Resources	New Construction
Academic Support Services	Budget Planning	Facilities Renewal/ Renovation
Student Support Services	Investment Strategies	Technology
Residence Life	Fund-raising/Development	Campus Infrastructure

---

9. Ibid. 143–50.

As authors of this book, we take a holistic view of planning. It is our view that planning at a college or university falls within three broad areas, as outlined in figure 2.1.

While figure 2.1 displays three functional areas of planning, we emphasize that, where planning is most effective, the three areas are integrated and interdependent. Chapters 3–5 describe the essential elements that go into academic planning, resource planning, and facilities planning, respectively. The remainder of the volume focuses on the *integrated* nature of planning. Good planning is not done in silos. Indeed, we argue that academic planning is the engine that drives all other types of planning at a college or university. Budgets are not expended, people are not hired, and buildings are not constructed without a sense of purpose that is clearly rooted in the academic mission of the college or university as expressed in its teaching, research, and service.

Chapter 3

Academic Planning

We noted in chapter 2 that academic planning is the engine that drives all other planning at a college or university. It refers not only to curricular planning, but also to planning for adequate and appropriate academic and related administrative support and other services, and student support services. It must also reflect the institution's commitment to understanding and acting on results of assessments of its effectiveness and success.

Academic planning is rooted in fundamental questions that confront all institutions of higher education: Who are the constituencies that are to be served? What is the appropriate balance between and among instruction, research, and service at the institution? What types of students and faculty does the institution seek to attract, and what are the appropriate programs, services, support personnel, and physical facilities that are needed to ensure that the institution attracts and retains those students and faculty? Also important are questions such as: What is the best way to reach and engage students, faculty, and others that the institution wishes to attract? How does the institution judge success, and how does it make use of information about the level of success that is attained/ sustained? In this chapter, we explore how a variety of institutions have answered such questions, and in so doing

we also explore how they have engaged in academic planning.

Academic planning is grounded in an institution's mission. Consequently, effectively articulating that mission is the first step in effective planning. A good mission statement has broad consensus within the institutional community that grows out of comprehensive discussion concerning the institution's central purposes. As we mentioned in chapter 2, George Keller noted that it is not a presidential vision statement, nor is it a policy directive from the board of trustees. It is a carefully reasoned analysis of what an institution aspires to be and the core values that it embraces. Mission statements should be more than simple clichés that promise, for example, that "students and faculty will interact in a rich intellectual environment in which each individual has the opportunity to achieve his or her full potential." While a noble sentiment, this statement tells us nothing about the institution's purposes and priorities. A mission statement must speak to central issues at a college or university, such as the balance between undergraduate and graduate education; the balance between the liberal arts and technical and professional programs; and the relative emphasis on teaching, research, and public service. It is characterized by a sense of vision that, while not immutable, nonetheless represents a long-term statement of institutional values around which human and fiscal resource allocation decisions can be made. While responsive to the institution's ever-changing external environment, mission statements should not be whimsical, morphing with each new trend that emerges. Instead, the best mission statements typically are the product of broad-based conversations across the spectrum of constituencies that comprise a campus—faculty, to be sure, but also administrative and professional staff, clerical staff, representative groups from the student body, and perhaps alumni and friends of the institution. As noted earlier, a mission statement should represent consensus as to what the institution wants to be and the long-term direction in which it is headed.

Consider the following mission statement for the University of Delaware, which clearly states the institution's values and priorities.

> Chartered as a college in 1833, the University of Delaware has evolved into a comprehensive land-grant, sea-grant, space-grant, and urban-grant institution. The University stands for excellence in the education of its undergraduate and graduate students, in scholarship, and in service to its state and to society. The relative emphasis placed on these three elements varies among units, yet all share responsibility in each. To accomplish its mission, the University maintains an environment where creativity, critical thinking, free inquiry, and respect for the views and values of others flourish. University governance

is conducted in a spirit of openness and cooperative interaction among trustees, administrators, faculty, staff, and students. The University strives to make all people feel welcome, regardless of their cultural, ethnic, or religious backgrounds, or of their race, color, age, gender, or sexual preference. Balance between the liberal arts and technical and professionally oriented disciplines, and between undergraduate and graduate education, is a university goal.

The University reaffirms its historic mission to provide the highest quality education for its undergraduate students. The faculty are responsible for helping students learn to reason critically and independently, gain knowledge of the diverse culture and environment in which they live, and develop into well-informed citizens and leaders. To accomplish these goals, the University provides a learning setting enriched by undergraduate student research, experiential learning, and study-abroad programs. The University places high priority on the education of qualified Delaware residents and provides opportunity for a diverse group of citizens to participate in postsecondary education. Since the University is located in a state with a small population, providing programs of quality and diversity requires a community of student-scholars that reaches beyond the boundaries of the state, one that reflects the nation's racial and cultural diversity.

The University of Delaware also aspires to excellence in graduate education, the heart of which is scholarship and research. The creation, application, and communication of knowledge is a primary goal of the institution and of every faculty member, providing the substance for creative, informed teaching. Research is typically based on cooperation between faculty and students, whereby faculty mentors teach students to conduct independent research and to master problem-solving techniques. Through involvement of undergraduates in faculty research, the University creates a special bond between its undergraduate and graduate programs.

The University is also committed to providing service to society, especially in Delaware and the neighboring region. Public service is a responsibility of every academic unit. In addition, each faculty member is responsible for service to the University community and to his or her profession. The University emphasizes practical research, provides extension services, and works to solve problems confronting the community.

The University of Delaware is an intellectual and cultural center for its community and for the citizens of Delaware and the surrounding region, providing lectures, exhibits, performances, and athletic events and facilities. Central to the scholarly and intellectual life of the campus is the University Library, a resource for both the University and the state.

Excellence requires selectivity and focus. Institutional vitality depends on maintaining and building from existing strengths and judging new proposals according to the University's resource base and mission. Priority is given to programs that meet the needs of society, in particular those of the state and surrounding community, or programs that build on the institution's particular strengths and demonstrated excellence. In the development of graduate and research programs, the University will continue to reflect the state's and the region's globally-oriented economic base, its internationally recognized cultural institutions, and its particular geographical, social, and ecological environment.[10]

In chapter 6, "Understanding the Language of Planning," we present a more detailed discussion of developing the institutional mission statement, planning goals derived therefrom, and measurable planning objectives that provide clear markers for assessing progress in meeting those planning goals.

Our focus in this chapter is on four basic questions that academic planning is intended to answer:

- Who is the intended market?
- What programs and services are needed to serve that market adequately and appropriately?
- What image or "brand" does the institution wish to project to the market?
- How will the institution know if it is successful?

10. University of Delaware, Self-Study Report for Middle States Higher Education Commission (Newark, DE: University of Delaware, unpublished manuscript, 2001).

The form of these questions may not seem familiar to or make comfortable many in higher education because of the "business" orientation, but the content describes a structured/disciplined way of thinking about the programs and services an institution offers.

Who is the intended market?

Answering this question is more complicated than it might seem at first blush. This is particularly evident as one navigates the generally understood categories of institutions. For example, it is arguable that the primary market for baccalaureate-granting colleges is high school students intent on pursuing a degree in the liberal arts and sciences. This is very much the case for schools such as Amherst College in Massachusetts, Rhodes College in Tennessee, and Reed College in Oregon. The intended market is evident in the text on each institution's Web site. Amherst President Anthony W. Marx states the following:

> Our responsibility remains to select the best of diverse students, so that they may come here and learn from each other. To ensure that they balance learning and effort of mind, spirit, talent and body. To fire in them a lifelong desire for learning and moral reasoning and action. To inspire them to do what the college was founded for—to enlighten, care for and advance society as a whole, within and beyond our borders.

> It remains our students' responsibility to learn, engage and change the world. It remains the faculty's to inform teaching with scholarship that is deep but also broad—in the way it can be only at a great liberal arts college. And it remains our duty, together, to serve the community, and thereby learn further; to work with those less privileged. By serving our core mission of education, we serve beyond it.[11]

Rhodes College characterizes its vision as follows:

> Rhodes College aspires to graduate students with a life-long passion for learning, a compassion for others, and the ability to translate academic study and personal concern into effective leadership and action in their communities and the world. We will achieve our aspiration through four strategic imperatives:

> **1. Student Access**
> To attract and retain a talented, diverse student body and engage these students in a challenging, inclusive and culturally-broadening college experience.

> **2. Student Learning**
> To ensure our faculty and staff have the talent, the time and the resources to inspire and involve our students in meaningful study, research and service.

> **3. Student Engagement**
> To enhance student opportunities for learning in Memphis.

> **4. Student Inspiration**
> To provide a residential place of

11. Anthony W. Marx, "Inauguration Address," remarks of the president, Amherst College, Amherst, MA, October 26, 2003, www.amherst.edu/news/inauguration/address.html.

learning that inspires integrity and high achievement through its beauty, its emphasis on values, its Presbyterian history, and its heritage as a leader in the liberal arts and sciences.[12]

And Reed College describes itself in the following manner:

Since its founding in 1908 as an independent undergraduate institution, Reed College, in Portland, Oregon, has remained steadfast to one central commitment: to provide a balanced, comprehensive education in liberal arts and sciences, fulfilling the highest standards of intellectual excellence. The distinctive Reed experience includes a challenging curriculum involving wide reading, conference and laboratory-based teaching in small groups, and a student body motivated by enthusiasm for serious intellectual work. Reed offers a B.A. in one of 22 major fields and numerous interdisciplinary fields, as well as a master of arts in liberal studies degree.[13]

In each instance, the college focuses on the intellectual development of undergraduate students through high-quality instruction and a campus life that fosters learning both in and out of the classroom. The emphasis is clearly and exclusively on teaching and learning.

Moving from baccalaureate institutions to master's institutions, a discernable market shift is evident. These colleges and universities are what were formerly referred to as comprehensive institutions—primarily undergraduate instruction, with some graduate instruction in selected professional fields. Indeed, many of these institutions have their origins as teacher training institutions. To illustrate the shift in market emphasis, consider the following values statements from the Web site of California State University, Northridge:

1. Commitment to Teaching, Scholarship, and Active Learning. We demonstrate excellence in teaching. We honor and reward high performance in learning, teaching, scholarship, research, service, and creative activity. Because the quality of our academic programs is central to our mission, we encourage intellectual curiosity and protect the multiple expressions of academic freedom.

2. Commitment to Excellence. We set the highest standards for ourselves in all of our actions and activities and support the professional development of faculty, staff and administrators. We assess our performance so that every area of University life will be continually improved and renewed. We recognize and reward our efforts of greatest distinction and through them provide state and national leadership.

3. Respect for All People. We aspire to behave as an inclusive, cooperative community. Our behaviors, policies,

12. Rhodes College, "Rhodes Vision," Memphis, www.rhodes.edu/AboutRhodes/RhodesVIsion/index.cfm.

13. Reed College, "About Reed: Mission and History: About Reed College," Portland, OR, web.reed.edu/about_reed/history.html.

and programs affirm the worth and personal dignity of every member of the University community and contribute to a campus climate of civility, collegiality, tolerance, and reasoned debate.

4. Alliances with the Community. We seek partnerships with local schools, community colleges, businesses, government and social agencies to advance the educational, intellectual, artistic, civic, cultural and economic aspirations of our surrounding communities.

5. Encouragement of Innovation, Experimentation, and Creativity. We seek to provide an environment conducive to innovation, experimentation, and creativity. We encourage all members of our community to take intellectual and creative risks and to embrace changes that will enhance the fulfillment of the University's mission.[14]

Where the market for baccalaureate colleges focuses mainly on teaching and learning, the market is wider at master's degree institutions. Here, the focus includes graduate education and students interested in pursuing master's-level study, most often in education and business, but frequently in other disciplines as well. The introduction of the terms "research," "service," and "creative activity" indicate that master's institutions much more frequently include within their market context agencies dealing with contracts and grants as well as other community/

outreach contacts. The fourth item within the values statement explicitly addresses partnerships with schools and community colleges (for both student recruitment and placement of graduates) as well as business, government, and social agencies (reflecting curriculum within professional programs).

Comparable language can be seen in the vision and mission statements of West Chester University of Pennsylvania, as they appear on the university's Web site:

Vision Statement
West Chester University will be a national model for excellence for public regional comprehensive universities and especially noted for:

• Undergraduate programs that actively engage students in connecting the life of the mind to the world in which they live and work.

• The responsiveness of its graduate and post-baccalaureate programs to regional needs.

• Its focus on providing lifelong-learning, technical, and applied skills essential to graduates' success now and in the future.

• A commitment by faculty, staff, and administrators to provide access and to serve effectively the educational needs of a diverse student body.

• Its role as a leading educational and cultural resource and partner in fostering the economic, social,

14. California State University, Northridge, "Mission, Values, and Vision: Values," Northridge, CA, www.csun.edu/academic.affairs/csunmission.htm.

and cultural vitality of southeastern Pennsylvania. [15]

The West Chester University Mission Statement

West Chester University, a member of the Pennsylvania State System of Higher Education, is a public, regional, comprehensive institution committed to providing access and offering high-quality undergraduate education, select post-baccalaureate and graduate programs, and a variety of educational and cultural resources for its students, alumni, and citizens of southeastern Pennsylvania."

Again, the language used at this master's institution defines a student market that is primarily undergraduate, but also targets graduate students in selected academic programs. And like California State University, Northridge, West Chester University is broadening its market outreach by defining itself as an educational and cultural resource in the community and a partner in fostering the sustainable development (i.e., economic, social, and cultural vitality) of the region.

Not surprising, research/doctoral universities address a complex set of markets, as exemplified in the mission statement of Iowa State University:

Mission Statement

Iowa State University of Science and Technology is a public land-grant institution serving the people of Iowa, the nation, and the world through its interrelated programs of instruction, research, extension, and professional service. With an institutional emphasis upon areas related to science and technology, the University carries out its traditional mission of discovering, developing, disseminating, and preserving knowledge.

Iowa State University provides high quality undergraduate programs across a broad range of disciplines, as befits the institution's stature as a university. In its dedication to excellence in learning, the University strives to instill in its students the discernment, intellectual curiosity, knowledge and skills essential for their individual development and their useful contribution to society. A common goal of undergraduate education is to assure that all students, regardless of disciplinary major, acquire literacy in science and technology, an understanding of humane and ethical values, an awareness of the intellectual, historical, and artistic foundations of our culture, and a sensitivity to other cultures and to international concerns. Consonant with its role as a teaching and research institution, Iowa State University has a strong commitment to graduate education that, at both the master's and doctoral levels, emphasizes the development of professional, research, and scholarship skills.

As an integral part of the learning process, Iowa State University fosters the discovery and dissemination of new knowledge by supporting research, scholarship, and creative activity. The University also uses

15. West Chester University, "WCU Vision, Mission & Values Statements," West Chester, PA, www.wcupa.edu/_INFORMATION/FACTS.WCU/mission.htm.

existing knowledge to address problems and issues of concern to the state of Iowa in particular, as well as to the national and global community. The University's endeavors in discovery and innovation are supported by public and private resources and are conducted in an environment of open scientific inquiry and academic freedom.

Engagement through extension, professional service, and continuing education activities is achieved through innovative and effective outreach programs that provide the people of Iowa, and beyond, with practical knowledge and information derived from leading discovery, innovation, and learning/instructional efforts at Iowa State University and elsewhere. Through engagement, the University stimulates and encourages progressive change.

Iowa State University enrolls academically qualified students who represent diverse age groups, socio-economic levels, racial ancestries, ethnic heritages, and international cultures, and who provide a gender balance. Through the use of a variety of educational opportunities, advanced instructional technologies, and student services, the University supports the development of both traditional and non-traditional students, preparing them for citizenship and life-long learning in a rapidly changing world.

Finally, Iowa State University participates in international efforts to alleviate world hunger and poverty, to prepare students and faculty to be productive and responsible citizens of the world, and to contribute to increased cultural, educational, economic, scientific, and socio-political interchange and understanding between and among Iowans and other members of the world community.[16]

The scope of this mission statement is not atypical for land grant universities. In addition to targeting undergraduate and graduate students across a broad range of academic disciplines, the introduction of Ph.D.-granting activity on a large scale means the concomitant introduction of research and service activity on a similarly large scale. Research is both pure and applied, and represents contractual and grant relationships with governmental agencies and businesses not just in the state, but nationally and internationally. The land grant component of the institutional mission represents a special relationship with the agricultural community at both the state and national level. The broad range of teaching, research, and service activity attracts students not only from Iowa and the forty-nine other states, but from throughout the world. As the result, the institution markets itself internationally. The complex nature of the research/doctoral university market is explained more fully in Iowa State University's assessment of its multiple roles:

- Iowa State University must strive to develop and maintain learning,

16. Iowa State University, "Mission Statement and Role Statement," Ames, IA, www.iastate.edu/~president/plan/2005/mission.html.

discovery, and engagement programs that fulfill the responsibilities of a major land-grant institution.

- Iowa State University shares with the other public institutions of higher education within Iowa the joint responsibility of providing a full range of high quality educational opportunities. Coordination among these institutions with respect to programs, clientele, and geographic areas is necessary to ensure that the priority needs of all Iowans are addressed and to avoid unnecessary duplication.

- Iowa State has a statewide system for extension education and information dissemination.

- Iowa State continues to be a leading higher education institution with institutional emphasis on science and technology.

- Consistent with its historic role, Iowa State University contributes to the economic development of the state of Iowa by attracting public and private organizations seeking proximity to leading authorities in particular fields, by participating in technology transfer, and by assisting efforts to strengthen and diversify the economic base of Iowa.

- Iowa State University assumes responsibility for helping to protect, maintain and improve Iowa's natural resources through the discovery and diffusion of knowledge and technology. [17]

The complexity of the market for

research/doctoral universities is by no means restricted to land grant institutions. Consider Duke University's mission statement:

James B. Duke's founding Indenture of Duke University directed the members of the University to "provide real leadership in the educational world" by choosing individuals of "outstanding character, ability and vision" to serve as its officers, trustees and faculty; by carefully selecting students of "character, determination and application;" and by pursuing those areas of teaching and scholarship that would "most help to develop our resources, increase our wisdom, and promote human happiness."

To these ends, the mission of Duke University is to provide a superior liberal education to undergraduate students, attending not only to their intellectual growth but also to their development as adults committed to high ethical standards and full participation as leaders in their communities; to prepare future members of the learned professions for lives of skilled and ethical service by providing excellent graduate and professional education; to advance the frontiers of knowledge and contribute boldly to the international community of scholarship; to promote an intellectual environment built on a commitment to free and open inquiry; to help those who suffer, cure disease, and promote health, through sophisticated medical research and thoughtful patient care; to provide wide ranging educational opportunities,

17. Ibid.

on and beyond our campuses, for traditional students, active professionals and life-long learners using the power of information technologies; and to promote a deep appreciation for the range of human difference and potential, a sense of the obligations and rewards of citizenship, and a commitment to learning, freedom and truth.

By pursuing these objectives with vision and integrity, Duke University seeks to engage the mind, elevate the spirit, and stimulate the best effort of all who are associated with the University; to contribute in diverse ways to the local community, the state, the nation and the world; and to attain and maintain a place of real leadership in all that we do.[18]

Absent the land grant component of marketplace, Duke University's market emphasis is no less complex than that of Iowa State University. In addition to an undergraduate curriculum, Duke University seeks to provide "excellent graduate and professional education" and research and service activity that will "contribute boldly to the international community of scholarship," and it identifies a particular market niche in "sophisticated medical research and thoughtful patient care."

Turning to two-year community colleges, one might expect a simpler marketplace—students interested in completing lower-division undergraduate study leading to the associate's degree and perhaps transfer to an upper-division

institution. While this is a component of many community colleges' markets, it is by no means the sole niche. Consider the following vision statement for Johnson County Community College (JCCC) in Overland Park, Kansas:

> The vision, mission and values of JCCC were adopted in 1999.

Vision
JCCC will enhance its leadership role among community colleges in the United States. The college will continue to enrich the quality of life for those it serves through creative solutions to educational, economic, and community challenges.

September 23, 1999
Mission
Learning comes first at JCCC. The college:

- delivers lifelong educational programs and services that are convenient and accessible

- provides professional training opportunities

- provides opportunities for personal growth and cultural enrichment

- maintains a caring, supportive environment

- stimulates economic development

- is accountable to its stakeholders

September 23, 1999
Values
As an institution of higher education, Johnson County Community College supports a statement of values identified

18. Duke University, "The Mission of Duke University," Durham, NC, www.planning.duke.edu/mission.html.

by the Carnegie Commission as applicable and enduring for all communities of learning. More specifically, we believe that Johnson County Community College should be:

- a place where all faculty, students, and staff share goals and work together to strengthen teaching and learning;

- a place where freedom of expression and civility are practiced, encouraged, and protected among all groups;

- a place where every person is respected and where diversity is pursued;

- a place where individuals accept their obligations to the group and where well-defined governance processes guide behavior for the good of the institution;

- a place where the well being of each member is supported and where service to others, internally and externally, is encouraged;

- a place whose ideas and resources are shared with other members of the educational community— locally, regionally, nationally, and internationally; and

- a place in which the institution's rituals, affirming both tradition and change, are shared and where the accomplishments of its staff and students are recognized.[19]

In defining its student marketplace, JCCC clearly identifies degree-seeking students, but also addresses the fact that many community college students have needs other than degree completion— e.g., vocational certifications, specific technology training needs, and personal enrichment.

With funding coming from local government and contracts with local businesses and industry, community colleges—perhaps even more than their four-year counterparts—must understand the needs of the local marketplace and be as responsive as possible to those needs. While JCCC is a large two-year institution with a credit-headcount enrollment in excess of 18,000, the facets of the two-year community college market evidenced at JCCC are also present in smaller institutions. Northwestern Connecticut Community College (NCCC) enrolls just over 1,500 students and characterizes its mission as follows:

> The main mission of NCCC is to provide higher education to students who are interested in pursuing postsecondary study. As part of the system of state-funded community and technical colleges, Northwestern offers academic programs of high standard and moderate cost to students who may have varied educational goals. Occupational training, transfer, and general study are among the reasons students attend Northwestern; the College also offers other educational opportunities to both the community and individuals. In general, the College endeavors to provide the education and

19. Johnson County Community College, "The Vision, Mission and Values of JCCC," Overland Park, KS, www.jccc.net/home/site/welcome/tocaboutjccc/missionall.

services its students wish to have.[20]

While more brief than the JCCC articulation of market, NCCC's mission has captured common elements—a student body with diverse instructional needs and the necessity for outreach to the community. That outreach is clearly defined through NCCC's continuing and extended studies that address, among other things, business and workforce development, and personal and professional development within the community.

It is obvious from the foregoing discussion that the breadth and depth of institutional market correlates strongly with institutional classification/type. However, it is important to remember that the factors that shape a college's or university's Carnegie Classification are deliberate institutional choices that should be the product of careful planning. Those planning choices go beyond simply defining the institution as baccalaureate, master's, or research/doctoral.

For example, what sort of undergraduate students does the institution seek to attract? Amherst College states that it seeks "to select the best of diverse students." The college's Web site profiles the class of 2008 as follows: the average SAT score is 1443, 35 percent are

students of color, and 6 percent are non-U.S. citizens.[21] The college has identified what might be characterized as the high-end of the traditional-age undergraduate student marketplace and is clearly successful in that market. However, the segment of the admissions marketplace that exhibits those characteristics is somewhat narrow.

Other institutions make different decisions based upon their mission and vision. For example, the University of Massachusetts Boston is an urban institution committed to addressing the educational needs of the greater Boston area. Its fact sheet cites the following characteristics of its student market in fall 2004:

- The mean SAT score for enrolling freshmen is 1039.

- Fifty-nine percent of undergraduates are first-generation college students. Approximately 400 are veterans.

- The median age of undergraduate students is 24.

- Students of color make up 37 percent of undergraduate enrollment.

- About 69 percent of all students report working 11 or more hours in a typical week, and about 27 percent report working more than 30 hours. Thirty-one percent of seniors report working more

20. Northwestern Connecticut Community College, "Mission Statement," Winsted, CT, documentation previously available on the web as of fall 2005.

21. Amherst College, "First-Year Students in the Class of 2008 in the Fifty-Eighth Annual Report to Secondary Schools," Amherst, MA, www.amherst.edu/admission/process/ssr08.pdf.

than 30 hours per week.[22]

The University of Massachusetts Boston has clearly defined a market for itself that is dramatically different from that of Amherst College. It is, in no small measure, a nontraditional student body comprising older students from families with little or no history of college attendance, who have not attained SAT scores that are as high and may be less academically talented, and who, in addition to studying, spend considerable time working. The University of Massachusetts Boston's student market reflects its tradition and history as an urban institution, just as Amherst College's market reflects its tradition and history as a highly selective, traditional liberal arts college. *One market type is not better than the other—both reflect conscious choices to reflect institutional mission.* But as we will discuss, the deliberate definition of market carries with it the need to define appropriate academic and student support services that reflect the intellectual and social needs of each respective market.

Other types of market decisions carry similarly important consequences. As institutions opt to move into the graduate student marketplace, other decisions come into play. Graduate instruction requires greater amounts of faculty scholarship, measured in terms of research and service activity. As faculty members engage in research

and service and supervision of graduate students, what are the implications for undergraduate instruction? What sorts of institutional and administrative services are needed to support graduate teaching, research, and public service? What sorts of external linkages and partnerships are essential to sustaining quality within the graduate program? These are important planning questions for institutions introducing master's-level instruction and intensify geometrically in the doctoral study component of research/doctoral universities.

A caution is in order before leaving the discussion of institutional markets. Any decision with respect to defining the marketplace to be served—especially where the decision involves expansion of that market—*must* be firmly rooted in a college's or university's mission if planning is to be successful. As technology rapidly evolves and demand for distance education increases, particularly in the areas of graduate and professional education, there is the temptation to rush into new markets. This is especially true for tuition-dependent institutions experiencing financial stress. However, careful planning requires a methodical cost-benefit analysis of any institutional market expansion.

Graduate and professional education, in and of itself, has recurring resource requirements not just for teaching, but for associated research and service

22. University of Massachusetts Boston, "Who Are Our Students?" Boston, MA, unpublished documentation on fall 2004 enrollment previously available on the web as of fall 2005.

activity. While contracts and grants are defined as an institutional revenue stream, there are few, if any, institutions that claim that research and public service are money-making propositions, especially in light of the administrative and institutional overhead needed to sustain them. Fold in the technology costs associated with virtual delivery of graduate and professional education, and it is immediately evident that any market expansion must be a carefully reasoned, thoroughly cost-estimated decision that is consistent with an institution's overall mission.

What programs and services are needed to serve that market adequately and appropriately?

As we noted earlier, careful definition of market niche for a college or university should be accompanied by a reasoned analysis of the programs and services necessary to support and serve that market niche adequately. Consider again, Amherst College, a highly selective baccalaureate institution that accepts a fraction of its applicant pool and typically admits a freshman class that has average SAT scores exceeding 1400. What sorts of support services are required for such academically able students? Peer tutoring and academic writing services are two prominently listed services on the Amherst College Web site. Here is how the college characterizes peer tutoring:

Peer Tutoring is available to students who are enrolled in Amherst courses and for a variety of reasons find themselves in need of tutorial assistance. Peer Tutors are approved by faculty in the following disciplines: Astronomy, Biology, Chemistry, Chinese, Computer Science, Economics, French, Geology, German, Greek, Japanese, Latin, Mathematics, Music, Philosophy, Physics, Psychology, Russian and Spanish. As is customary, students who are concerned about their academic performance are advised to discuss their concerns with the professor in the course. Those who are interested in working with Peer Tutors must first receive the approval of their professors. Peer Tutor assignments are made in consultation with [the] Director of Tutorial Services… She is available for short-term counseling sessions that help students address problems that impede academic progress, i.e., procrastination, time mismanagement, competing priorities (academic and social) and related issues…

The Quantitative Skills Center provides walk-in tutorial services. Faculty-approved tutors are available to work with students who want to improve their conceptual understanding in math, science, and economics courses. The Quantitative Fellow works with students who want to fortify study habits and improve problem-solving skills.[23]

Peer tutoring at Amherst College is clearly designed to enhance academic performance. It is by no means remedial or intended to provide basic skills.

23. Amherst College, "Services for Academic Support," Amherst, MA, www.amherst.edu/~dos/acadsupport.html.

The following is a description of the Academic Writing Services: "The staff of the Writing Center helps students at any stage of the writing process: getting started, organizing papers, clarifying prose, correcting grammatical glitches, and coping with anxiety about writing."[24]

Again, the focus is not on remediation in basic grammar and spelling. Academic Writing Services is a program designed to help academically gifted students become *better* writers. Both the peer tutoring and writing services are carefully developed academic support programs that are geared to the market sector that Amherst College attracts. These services are clearly appropriate for that market, but would be totally unsuited for an institution that targets a different market.

Consider Delaware Valley College in Pennsylvania. Like Amherst College, it is an independent, baccalaureate institution, but it has defined a different admissions market segment for itself. Where Amherst accepts less than 20 percent of its applicant pool, Delaware Valley College accepts more than 80 percent of its applicants.[25] With less selective admissions criteria, Delaware Valley College freshmen have a lower academic profile than Amherst College freshmen (SAT scores average 1000 at Delaware Valley College compared with 1400 and over at Amherst College).

Academic support services at Delaware Valley College are designed to support the educational needs of that market niche and, not surprisingly, look different from those at Amherst College. Consider the CHOICES Program available at Delaware Valley College and described as follows on its Web site:

> Sometimes not every student is equally prepared to start college. The CHOICES Program's purpose is to help first year students strengthen their academic foundations while adjusting to college life in a supportive environment.
>
> The CHOICES Program is open to a select number of motivated first year students that are interested in obtaining new skills to increase their academic performance. Students accepted into the CHOICES Program enter Delaware Valley College as a CHOICES major and upon successful completion of their first year, apply to their prospective major.
>
> What does CHOICES offer?
>
> - **PERSONALIZED CURRICULUM**
>   Students will work closely with our CHOICES Coordinator to create a class schedule structured for successful and integrated learning.
>
> - **REDUCED ACADEMIC LOAD**
>   A strong academic foundation helps ensure a strong academic future. Academic courses are specifically balanced first and second semester to make your adjustment to college more

---

24. Ibid.

25. Delaware Valley College, "Profile of the Class of 2007," Doylestown, PA, www.devalcol.edu/services/research/downloads/profiles/2003.pdf.

manageable.

- **ACADEMIC SERVICES**
  CHOICES students have access to a full range of academic support services including academic advising, tutoring, learning support and counseling services. This is in addition to their progress being closely monitored by the CHOICES Coordinator during the freshman year.

It is possible that students admitted to Delaware Valley College under these provisions may require more than eight semesters of study to qualify for graduation.

Learning Strategies and CHOICES Seminar

Every CHOICES program student is required to take the Learning Strategies course in the Fall semester and CHOICES Seminar in the Spring semester.

The combination of both classes will supply each student with the tools needed for a successful college experience. The CHOICES Seminar is only available to CHOICES students.

These courses have been specifically selected to assist each student with identifying and building upon various academic and personal strengths.

Some focal points include:

- Accessing College Resources
- Active Reading
- Career Exploration
- Critical Thinking
- Learning Style Assessment
- Note Taking
- Personal Academic Responsibilities
- Stress Management
- Test Taking
- Time Management

The CHOICES Program provides the expertise and resources designed to reinforce the student's educational foundation and strengthen academic skills. Participation in the CHOICES Program signifies the students' commitment to their education, their future, and their own personal success.

The Counseling and Learning Support Department provides the Delaware Valley College community with numerous programs and services to assist every student. In addition to the CHOICES Program, we offer Tutoring in the Learning Center, Personal Counseling, the ACT 101 Program and Learning Support Services.[26]

The CHOICES Program is clearly a carefully planned, well-thought-out academic strategy for enhancing the prospect of success for college freshmen who exhibit promise, but who may not have in place all of the requisite skills at the level necessary for successful undergraduate study. The college clearly

26. Delaware Valley College, "Counseling & Learning Support Services," Doylestown, PA. www.devalcol.edu/counseling/archive/services_choices.html.

understands the market niche that it draws from and has crafted appropriate support services for that market place. A comparably successful support program is Delaware Valley College's ACT 101 Program, supported by state funds and targeted specifically to Pennsylvania residents. It is described as follows:

What is Act 101?

The Higher Education Equal Opportunity Program (ACT 101) was established by the Commonwealth of Pennsylvania in 1971. Institutions participating in the program recruit highly motivated students who show the potential to succeed in college, with additional support (counseling and tutoring). The goal of ACT 101 is to help these institutions provide opportunities for both traditional and non-traditional students seeking a college education.

Who is Eligible?

ACT 101 participants are chosen on the basis of their academic potential and motivation. To be eligible for program services, students must be full-time residents of Pennsylvania and must meet certain economic criteria.

Counseling Services

Counseling services are fundamental to the ACT 101 program. The program provides counseling services that assist students in realizing their personal and educational goals. The ACT 101 counselors work individually or in groups to provide help in the following areas:

- Personal counseling/crisis intervention

- Orientation to college and the ACT 101 program

- Assistance in career planning and decision making

- Assistance in values clarification and self-concept development

- Financial aid counseling

- Monitoring of student progress

- Lounge and Resource Center that provides computer station, photocopying, study area, TV/VCR, and textbook library

Tutorial Services

The ACT 101 program includes a strong tutorial component. The tutoring services are available on a walk-in basis or by appointment for all ACT 101 students. The tutorial coordinator works individually or in groups to provide help in the following areas:

- Basic skills in reading and writing

- Organizing study groups

- Individualized help with specific courses

- Study skills courses and workshops

- Time Management

Summer Program

ACT 101 provides a special summer component to all incoming freshmen. Services include tutoring and counseling, with an emphasis on time management, study skills, adjustment to college life, and information on campus and community. The summer program is linked to a variety of ACT 101 activities that are offered throughout the academic year.

Cultural Activities Program

The program assists ACT 101 students in developing an awareness of the many cultural activities available in the Tri-state area. ACT 101 sponsors trips to plays, concerts, art exhibits, and historic sites.[27]

Again, the ACT 101 program illustrates careful planning on the part of Delaware Valley College in structuring academic support services specifically designed to serve the market niche from which it draws. The contrasting services made available by Amherst College and Delaware Valley College demonstrate two decidedly different institutions that have consciously chosen to serve very different market niches and, in so doing, have executed exemplary academic planning in addressing the needs of those market niches.

Planning for appropriate support services goes well beyond student learning. Where the University of Delaware is primarily a residential campus, its nearby neighbor, Temple University in Philadelphia, has a student population of which 70 percent live in nonuniversity housing. In structuring both learning strategies and student life services, each institution confronts specific planning opportunities and challenges.

A residential campus has the opportunity to use on-campus housing for more than simply providing students with a place to sleep. For example, the University of Delaware has created the Learning Integrated Freshman Experience, or

LIFE Program, which is characterized as follows:

> LIFE stands for Learning Integrated Freshman Experience, and is one of four FYEs [First Year Experiences]. This program was developed in 1998 to encourage learning communities organized around themes. This is referred to as a LIFE cluster. Each cluster member is enrolled in one or more courses plus a co-curricular course, UNIV 101, through the Office of Undergraduate Studies. The Office of Residence Life supports the program through collaboration with professionals, faculty and students involved in the program. Resident Assistants on LIFE floors work with the Peer Mentors assigned to the floor's cluster. The two are able to assist each other and the students and create living and learning environments both on the floor and in the classroom.[28]

The residence hall, within the context of the LIFE program, becomes more than living space; it is a learning community. The University of Delaware has extended this concept to develop special interest housing, in which students with common interests are housed together, with programming in the residence hall directed at those areas of common interest. Consider the following description of the Ray Street housing complex:

> Built in 1990, Ray Street is the newest complex at the University of Delaware.

27. Delaware Valley College, "Student Support Services: Our Services: ACT 101," Doylestown, PA, www.devalcol.edu/academics/counseling/services_act101.html.

28. University of Delaware, "Learning Integrated Freshman Experience," Newark, DE, www.udel.edu/reslife/students/life.html.

It is comprised of 3 buildings on Laird Campus, each housing approx. 115 students. There are 15 lounges, 3 laundry rooms, and 3 kitchens, throughout the buildings...

The Ray Street staff consists of 1 Resident Assistant per floor, 2 Hall Directors, and a Complex Coordinator. In 2005-2006 there will be 18 active Special Interest Communities, several LIFE clusters, a governing student body, the Ray Street Activities Council (RSAC) and the Ray Street Senate (programming allocations board). The 16 communities are:

- Farmhouse Community

- Eco-house Community

- Martin Luther King Jr. Humanities Community

- Music Community

- Sexuality and Gender Community

- Creative and Performing Arts Community

- Engineering Community

- Cuisine Community

- Healthy Living Community

- H. Norman Schwarzkopf Leadership Community

- Political Awareness Community

- Impact Service Learning Community

- Crafts Community

- Latin American Culture Community

- Cinematic Arts Community

- Asian Community

- Medical Awareness Community

- Entrepreneurial Community[29]

In addition to the special interest communities housed at Ray Street, undergraduates in the University Honors Program are housed together. Clearly, a residential complex affords unique opportunities for creative programming in support of student learning both in and out of the classroom.

On the other hand, an urban campus such as Temple University has unique learning opportunities that only a major city can afford. With more than 70 percent of undergraduates living off campus, the challenge for Temple University is to program out-of-classroom learning experiences in a common venue. The Student Center becomes a focal point for student development, and the Office of Student Activities characterizes its mission as follows:

Through the work of the Student Activities Departmental professional staff and the various student committees, organizations and workers, the Student Center is a "laboratory" where students can learn and develop leadership, programming, management, interpersonal skills and social responsibility. It therefore becomes an integral part of Temple University's educational environment. The Student Center is a building, an organization and

29. University of Delaware, "Special Interest Housing: Ray Street Complex," Newark, DE, www.udel.edu/reslife/students/sih.html.

a program; it provides services, facilities and educational and recreational activities that enhance the quality of student life within a diverse college community.[30]

Temple University has a broad array of student organizations that utilize the Student Center and other facilities on campus as a means of enriching intellectual and social growth. Moreover, the fact that most students do not live on campus has not precluded learning communities. The university has simply used the undergraduate curriculum as a vehicle for creating such communities. The following description is found on the Temple University Web site:

> A Learning Community consists of two or more courses, scheduled in a block, which students take together as a group. . .

> Learning Communities are ideal for freshmen, however, freshmen or transfer students with fewer than 60 credits can enroll. Learning Communities are available for students in most undergraduate schools and colleges. . .

> Award-winning faculty, popular courses, and the opportunity to get to know your peers and build a support network. All of this while satisfying CORE, college, or major requirements! . . .

> *Learning for the New Century* is a one-credit freshman seminar designed for students in University Studies, the College of Liberal Arts, or other academic programs who are interested in gaining

a better understanding of the academic and social components of college. [Note: Seminars are also offered in the Fox School of Business and Management, the School of Communications and Theater, and the College of Science and Technology.] Topics covered include: an introduction to college, getting to know your professors, test-taking strategies, career development, using the library, and time management. Seminars are available as part of individual Learning Communities or as separate courses.[31]

Temple University also has the luxury of using the city of Philadelphia as a teaching tool. Students in the university's Tyler School of Art have access to the Philadelphia Museum of Art, a world-class facility. Students in the Boyer College of Music and Dance are exposed to the Philadelphia Orchestra and the Pennsylvania Ballet. The multicultural nature of urban populations makes the city a perfect resource for all students at the institution.

The point to be underscored is that both the University of Delaware and Temple University have a clear sense of mission and have structured academic and student support services consistent with that mission and the students they serve.

At institutions with instructional missions that include graduate study, a different set of services not typically found at undergraduate institutions

30. Temple University, Mission of the Student Activities Department. Philadelphia, PA, www.temple.edu/SAC/index2.html.

31. Temple University, "The Learning Communities at Temple University," Philadelphia, PA, www.temple.edu/LC/lc_students.html.

becomes important. While most colleges and universities include offices for undergraduate admissions and financial aid that centrally coordinate admissions activity and the packaging of undergraduate financial assistance, structures may be different at institutions with graduate-level offerings. Faculty at the department level typically make decisions about the admission of specific graduate students and whether or not to award assistantship or fellowship aid. This may necessitate an office of graduate studies to provide general oversight and administration for graduate study. Resident graduate students are not usually housed with undergraduates, and this raises another set of service issues for which most institutions must plan.

Institutions that have extensive graduate programs, by definition, also have extensive research and service components in their mission to provide the necessary scholarly support for creation of new knowledge within the discipline. Research and service activity dictate planning for yet another range of services. Most research universities have offices of sponsored research charged with assisting faculty in identifying funding sources for research activity, negotiating indirect cost rates associated with contract and grant activity, monitoring and auditing research expenditures, overseeing the patenting of intellectual property, and other related tasks. Institutions with extensive service activity similarly have administrative offices to monitor contractual outreach

activity. Land grant institutions have cooperative extension units to oversee all aspects of research and service being performed under the auspices of the federal Hatch Act.

It is clear from the foregoing discussion that good academic planning is comprehensive. It begins with a clear, institution-wide understanding of institutional mission and market and requires the development of appropriate services that support full realization of that mission. With these components in place, we move to consideration of two additional questions underpinning academic planning.

What image or "brand" does the institution wish to project to the market?

The University of Delaware is a research/doctoral-extensive university. It enrolls more than 20,000 students and annually awards more than 3,000 bachelor's degrees, 600 to 700 master's degrees, and 150 to 200 doctorates. It attracts in excess of $100 million in contracts and grants for instruction, research, and service activity. In other words, it is a large, complex institution; it has a strong graduate/research component; and it fulfills all of the criteria for being research/doctoral extensive. How, then, does the university distinguish itself from other flagship, land grant universities in the region and the nation? What is the image or brand that the University of Delaware wants to project? Consider the following from the university's

Admissions Viewbook:

> The University of Delaware is a teaching university. With a ratio of 14 full-time undergraduate students to each faculty member, Delaware students will tell you that they truly know their teachers and advisors. Accessibility is the key word that pops up over and over again – through e-mail, between class appointments, for lunch on Main Street, at graduation celebrations – our faculty are there and committed to making a difference in the lives of our students. In addition to teaching, our faculty conduct research. Over 600 faculty members accept undergraduates as research assistants, giving talented, motivated students the opportunity to see and take part in what is happening on the front lines of discovery at the university today. Our excellent teaching quality is constantly enhanced through such University initiatives as the Center for Teaching Effectiveness.[32]

The decision to characterize itself as a teaching university was not arbitrary on the part of the University of Delaware. It was the result of careful research within the student marketplace. The university had a clear sense of its three-pronged mission of teaching, research, and service, and was organizationally structured to realize that mission. But how did potential students within the admissions marketplace perceive the institution? Research found that a good many of the students that the university wished to attract were put off by what

appeared to be a large, impersonal research university. The strategy in developing the "teaching university" tag line was to assure incoming undergraduates that, despite the size of the student body, the relationship with faculty was very personal, and that attending a university where research occurs presents intellectual opportunities and challenges that are not found elsewhere.

The university took the "teaching university" tag line and incorporated it into all of its communications with the admissions marketplace. This strategy, among a number of other factors, contributed to a growth in applications for admission from 13,000 in 1995 to well over 22,000 in 2005. Careful communication of how an institution wishes to be branded is an integral part of effective academic planning.

The College of New Jersey (TCNJ) provides another illustration of branding. As is the case with many public, master's-level comprehensive institutions, TCNJ traces its origins to a state-operated teacher training institution. It was named Trenton State College throughout the 1960s, 1970s, and 1980s. During the 1980s, however, when most state-operated comprehensive colleges scrambled for students by relaxing admissions standards, Trenton State College actually raised its admissions standards. The result was a student body

32. University of Delaware, "Teachers Who Teach," Newark, DE, www.udel.edu/admissions/viewbook/explore/teachers.html.

with a higher academic profile than was typical for that type of institution. How then, given its academic profile, could the college distinguish itself from other state colleges and position itself to compete with private institutions for high-ability undergraduates? The college scored a coup when *U.S. News & World Report* cited it in the mid-1990s as one of the top regional colleges in the United States, and in 1996, Trenton State College became The College of New Jersey.[33] TCNJ now effectively uses its name to appeal to a market niche that is the result of careful long-term planning.

This discussion about branding is relevant to nontraditional institutions as well. Suppose you had the notion that higher education is more than an altruistic, common-good enterprise. Suppose you had the notion that you could make money delivering higher education services. Suppose you had the extreme notion that you could form a corporation to do this that would be listed on the NASDAQ stock market? And how would you effectively compete with traditional colleges and universities that treat such entrepreneurship with disdain? Welcome to the world of the Apollo Group, parent corporation of the University of Phoenix. Hoover's, a Dunn and Bradstreet company providing information on businesses in the United States, characterizes the Apollo Group as

follows:

> Even the sun god needs a college degree these days. Apollo Group is a for-profit education company that provides programs tailored to working adults. Its University of Phoenix, with more than 200,000 students at some 100 learning centers and 50 campuses (including an online campus), is the US's largest private university. The university offers undergraduate and graduate degrees in such areas as business, education, nursing, and information technology.[34]

How does a university that is only 30 years old grow into a higher education institution that has awarded nearly 172,000 degrees? The answer is not surprising—by carefully selecting a market niche and carefully planning a branding campaign. The University of Phoenix selected as its market niche working adults who wished to pursue a degree for career advancement. Aggressively marketing itself as "The University for Working Adults," its Web site engages that market niche as follows:

> At University of Phoenix, you can earn your bachelor's, master's or doctoral degree any way you want to—on campus, online, or in certain areas using a combination of both, which we call FlexNet®. University of Phoenix has grown to be the nation's largest private university, specializing in the education of working adults by offering degree

---

33. The College of New Jersey, "History of the College," Trenton, NJ, www.tcnj.edu/%7Eccr/about/history.html.

34. Hoover's, Inc., "Apollo Group, Inc.," Austin, TX, www.hoovers.com/apollo-group/--ID__42338--/free-co-factsheet.xhtml.

programs that are highly relevant, accessible, and efficient…you can complete your degree no matter where you live, what hours you work, or how often you travel or relocate.[35]

That the University of Phoenix has been extraordinarily successful in its branding strategies and in capturing its intended market niche is evident from the fact that most discussions of adult education and distance learning at traditional colleges and universities invariably involve some recognition of competition with, or benchmarking against, the University of Phoenix. The university used classic business strategies in defining its marketplace and in the publicity campaign directed at that marketplace. Given its success, it is not surprising that the University of Phoenix business model has been adapted by more traditional institutions seeking to expand their higher education delivery systems.

These are but a few examples of higher education branding. The consistent message is one of knowing and understanding the market that an institution defines for itself and developing appropriate strategies for communicating with that market. These are not serendipitous activities; they are the product of careful institutional planning and, most especially, careful academic planning that drives institutional decisions and resource allocations. That leads us to a final question that underpins effective academic planning.

How will the institution know if it is successful?

All of the foregoing discussion of effective planning comes down to the following proposition—planning is effective only if an institution can provide demonstrable evidence that it has successfully done what it set out to do. In short, a college or university must be able to assess its overall institutional effectiveness, in general, and the outcomes of student learning, specifically, if it is to say that academic planning has been successful. Institutional effectiveness implies that instructional services, academic and student support services, and institutional administrative services are in place, with resources allocated in a manner to ensure student success. In addition, student success must be demonstrable. Clear evidence must be available that shows that students have *learned as* the result of their experience at a college or university, and this demonstration of learning should extend far beyond a simple distribution of grades in a set of courses.

We will devote substantial discussion in chapter 7 to strategies for assessing institutional effectiveness and student learning outcomes. At this point, however, it is useful to examine the type of assessment standards against which

---

35. University of Phoenix, "Description of the University of Phoenix," Phoenix, AZ, unpublished documentation previously available on the web as of fall 2005.

accredited colleges and universities are judged. For illustrative purposes, we use the standards for accreditation adopted by the Middle States Commission on Higher Education. However, it is important to note that in one form or another, the other regional accrediting bodies and many of the disciplinary accrediting agencies have comparable standards.

Let us begin with Middle States' accreditation standard 7 (2006 edition), which governs institutional assessment. "The institution has developed and implemented an assessment process that evaluates its overall effectiveness in achieving its mission and goals and its compliance with accreditation standards.[36]"

Beyond a simple statement of the standard, Middle States' *Characteristics of Excellence in Higher Education* offers a series of fundamental elements characterizing institutional assessment as well as representative analysis and evidence that might be presented to support that assessment. Relative to the standard addressing institutional assessment, Middle States offers the following:

An accredited institution is expected to possess or demonstrate the following attributes or activities:

- documented, organized, and sustained assessment process to evaluate and

improve the total range of programs and services; achievement of institutional mission, goals, and plans; and compliance with accreditation standards that meets the following criteria:

– a foundation in the institution's mission and clearly articulated institutional, unit-level, and program-level goals that encompass all programs, services, and initiatives and are appropriately integrated with one another (see Standards 1: Mission and Goals and 2: Planning, Resource Allocation, and Institutional Renewal);

– systematic, sustained, and thorough use of multiple qualitative and/or quantitative measures that:

• maximize the use of existing data and information;

• clearly and purposefully relate to the goals they are assessing;

• are of sufficient quality that results can be used with confidence to inform decisions;

– support and collaboration of faculty and administration;

– clear realistic guidelines and a timetable, supported by appropriate investment of institutional resources;

– sufficient simplicity, practicality, detail, and ownership to be sustainable;

– periodic evaluation of the effectiveness and comprehensiveness of the institution's assessment

36. Middle States Commission on Higher Education, Characteristics of Excellence in Higher Education: Eligibility Requirements and Standards for Accreditation (Philadelphia: Middle States Commission on Higher Education, 2006), 25.

process;

– evidence that assessment results are shared and discussed with appropriate constituents and used in institutional planning, resource allocation, and renewal (see Standard 2: Planning, Resource Allocation, and Institutional Renewal) to improve and gain efficiencies in programs, services and processes, including activities specific to the institution's mission (e.g., service, outreach, research); and

– written institutional (strategic) plan(s) that reflect(s) consideration of assessment results.[37]

As noted, the discussion goes on to suggest examples of analysis and evidence in support of institutional assessment:

Optional Analysis and Evidence
In addition to the evidence inherent within or necessary to document the fundamental elements above, the following, although not required, may facilitate the institution's own analysis relative to this accreditation standard:

– analysis of the institutional culture for assessing institutional effectiveness, including:

  • the views of faculty and administrators on assessment;

  • faculty and administrators' understanding of their roles in assessing institutional effectiveness;

  • campus-wide efforts to encourage, recognize, and value efforts to

assess institutional effectiveness and to improve programs and services;

– analysis of the quality and usefulness of institutional support for assessment efforts, including the quality and usefulness of:

  • written statements of expectations for assessment work;

  • policies and governance structures to support institutional assessment;

– administrative, technical, and financial support for institutional assessment activities;

– professional development opportunities and resources for faculty and staff to learn how to assess institutional effectiveness and how to use the results;

– clear, appropriate criteria for determining whether key institutional goals and objectives have been achieved;

– analysis of whether the institution has sufficient, convincing, written evidence that it is achieving its mission and its key institutional goals;

– analysis of results of surveys of students and other relevant groups;

– review of evaluations of special, mission driven programs or projects, with recommendations for improvement, and evidence of action based on recommendations;

– evidence that institutional assessment

37. Ibid., 28.

findings are used to:

- improve student success;

- review and improve programs and services;

- plan, conduct, and support professional development activities;

- assist in planning and budgeting for the provision of programs and services;

- support decisions about strategic goals, plans, and resource allocation;

- inform appropriate constituents about the institution and its programs;

 — evidence of renewal strategies, made in response to assessment results

[included also under Standard 2 Optional Analyses]; or

 — analysis of evidence that renewal strategies made in response to assessment results have had the desired effect in improving programs, services, and initiatives.[38]

The importance of this description of assessment of institutional effectiveness is that it largely demystifies what is needed to describe "success" at the institutional level.[39]

Measuring success clearly must reflect a college's or university's overall mission, goals, and objectives. In examining the array of organizational units, programs, and services at an institution, the focus is on planning, decision making, and resource allocations that support the full realization of mission and concomitant goals and objectives. In the final analysis, if a college or university is to truly measure success, it must do so to a lesser or greater extent, depending upon mission, in terms of student learning. It seems odd to ask whether students actually learn as the result of their college or university experience. However, this important issue has not been addressed systematically until relatively recently.

Learning here refers not to the regurgitation of facts on a final exam. It refers to enhanced quantitative and verbal skills, and the ability to reason critically, to synthesize complex ideas, and to demonstrate in measurable ways real cognitive gains and related changes in behavior. For example, if a higher education institution's mission is, in part, to produce graduates who have ethics and values to contribute to society, and this is operationalized through a commitment to increase student engagement in solutions to society's sustainable energy challenges, then learning should include changes in student attitudes, values, and behavior

---

38. Ibid., 29–30.

39. Note the following admonition from Middle States with respect to the examples of analyses and evidence provided in support of assessment of institutional effectiveness: This is not a check-list. The tools and strategies for assessing institutional effectiveness certainly can be drawn from this list. But it might well also be supplemented with additional tools and strategies.

regarding energy conservation.

Middle States offers accreditation Standard 14 (2006 edition) for assessing student learning outcomes: "Assessment of student learning demonstrates that, at graduation or other appropriate points, the institution's students have knowledge, skills, and competencies consistent with institutional and appropriate higher education goals.[40]"

The fundamental elements associated with this type of assessment articulate traits and activities that support assessment of student learning outcomes. Relative to this standard, an accredited institution is characterized by:

- clearly articulated statements of expected student learning outcomes (see Standard 11: Educational Offerings), at all levels (institution, degree/program, course) and for all programs that aim to foster student learning and development, that are:

  - appropriately integrated with one another;

  - consonant with the institution's mission; and

  - consonant with the standards of higher education and of the relevant disciplines;

- a documented, organized, and sustained assessment process to evaluate and improve student learning that meets the following criteria:

  - systematic, sustained, and thorough use of multiple qualitative and/or quantitative measures that:

  - maximize the use of existing data and information;

  - clearly and purposefully relate to the goals they are assessing;

  - are of sufficient quality that results can be used with confidence to inform decisions; and

  - include direct evidence of student learning;

  - support and collaboration of faculty and administration;

  - clear, realistic guidelines and timetable, supported by appropriate investment of institutional resources;

  - sufficient simplicity, practicality, detail, and ownership to be sustainable; and

  - periodic evaluation of the effectiveness and comprehensiveness of the institution's student learning assessment processes;

- assessment results that provide sufficient, convincing evidence that

  students are achieving key institutional and program learning outcomes;

- evidence that student learning assessment information is shared and

  discussed with appropriate constituents and is used to improve teaching and learning; and

---

40. Middle States Commission on Higher Education, Characteristics of Excellence in Higher Education: Eligibility Requirements and Standards for Accreditation (Philadelphia: Middle States Commission on Higher Education, 2006), 63.

- documented use of student learning assessment information as part of institutional assessment.[41]

If institutions are to satisfy this accreditation standard, an enormous amount of up-front academic planning must have occurred. The intended learning outcomes of a given course, the courses within a department, the departments within a school or college, and, where applicable, the schools or colleges within the larger institution, must all be tied to the overarching mission, goals, and objectives. For example, a course in urban studies at the University of Delaware must demonstrate more than learning within the cognitive domain of the course content. The course may also address the service-learning component of the mission of the School of Urban Affairs and Public Policy , the outreach component of the College of Human Services, Education and Public Policy, and the mission and goals of the larger land grant/urban grant institution. These linkages are not a function of chance; they must be intended and must be demonstrably imbedded within the overall institutional plan for assessing student learning outcomes. Moreover, the information gleaned from measuring the extent to which those intended outcomes are or are not being achieved constitute the basis for improving teaching and learning at the institution. In addition, the information gathered in assessing student

learning outcomes must be folded into the larger assessment of overall institutional effectiveness.

How, then, does an institution begin to develop a process for assessing student learning outcomes? Once again, Middle States offers guidance in the form of possible analyses and types of evidence:

> In addition to the evidence inherent within or necessary to document the fundamental elements above, the following, although not required, may facilitate the institution's own analysis relative to this accreditation standard:

- analysis of institutional support for student learning assessment efforts, including:

  – written statements of expectations for student learning assessment work;

  – policies and governance structures to support student learning assessment;

  – administrative, technical, and financial support for student learning assessment activities and for implementing changes resulting from assessment; and

  – professional development opportunities and resources for faculty to learn how to assess student learning, how to improve their curricula, and how to improve their teaching;

- analysis of the clarity and appropriateness of standards for determining whether key learning outcomes have been achieved;

41. Ibid. 66–67

- evidence of workable, regularized, collaborative institutional processes and protocols for ensuring the dissemination, analysis, discussion, and use of assessment results among all relevant constituents within a reasonable schedule;

- analysis of the use of student learning assessment findings to:

  - assist students in improving their learning;

  - improve pedagogies, curricula and instructional activities;

  - review and revise academic programs and support services;

  - plan, conduct, and support professional development activities;

  - assist in planning and budgeting for the provision of academic programs and services;

  - support other institutional assessment efforts (see Standard 7: Institutional Assessment) and decisions about strategic goals, plans, and resource allocation; and

  - inform appropriate constituents about the institution and its programs;

- analysis of evidence that improvements in teaching, curricula, and support made in response to assessment results have had the desired effect in improving teaching, learning, and the success of other activities;

- analysis of the institutional culture for assessing student learning, including:

  - the views of faculty and institutional leaders on assessment;

  - faculty members' understanding of their roles in assessing student learning;

  - the quality and usefulness of institutional support for student learning assessment efforts;

  - campus-wide efforts to encourage, recognize, and value efforts to assess student learning and to improve curricula and teaching;

  - evidence of collaboration in the development of statements of expected student learning and assessment strategies;

- evidence that information appropriate to the review of student retention, persistence, and attrition, is used to reflect whether these are consistent with student and institutional expectations [also included in Standard 8 Optional Analyses];

- evidence of the utilization of attrition information to ascertain characteristics of students who withdraw prior to attaining their educational objectives and, as appropriate, implementation of strategies to improve retention [also included under Optional Analyses in Standard 8];

- analysis of teaching evaluations, including identification of good practices; or

- analysis of course, department or school reports on classroom assessment

42. Ibid., 67–68.

practices and their outcomes, including grading approaches and consistency.[42]

Once again, the importance of this description is not its specific source, but its ability to demystify and frame institutional work on student learning outcomes assessment. As colleges and universities move forward in developing strategies to measure student learning outcomes and overall institutional effectiveness, it is important to ensure that a strong institutional research capability is resident within the institution. At larger, more complex schools, an office of institutional research is usually within the administrative structure. At smaller schools, the institutional research function may be distributed across offices such as admissions, registrar, and budget.

To sum up, regardless of institutional size and structure, it is important that the college have a clear understanding of its mission, goals, and objectives, and the *intended outcomes* therefrom. The extent to which those outcomes are being achieved constitutes the requisite measures of success for determining how effective academic planning has been and constitutes the baseline metrics for future academic planning.

Once a college or university has identified institutional markets consistent with its mission statement, appropriate support services for addressing the needs of those markets, and a branding strategy for reaching out to those markets, the institution must then ensure that appropriate human, fiscal, and physical resources are in place to fully service those markets. With a sense of what constitutes good academic planning, let us now turn to two other types of institutional planning that are largely driven by the academic plan, i.e., resource planning and facilities planning.

Chapter 4

Resource Planning

Planning documents are only as good as the financial and human resources that support them. An institution can write a wonderful mission statement, replete with appropriate goals and objectives. That same institution can define its marketplace and develop grand branding strategies. But unless human and fiscal resources are allocated in a fashion consistent with that overarching mission, goals, and objectives, all of the rest is but hollow rhetoric. Said another way, the institution's budget should represent a financial expression of mission and plans.

An institution can aspire to an academically talented student body or a student body that includes at-risk, first-generation students. In either instance, appropriate admission recruitment personnel; teaching, academic, and student support personnel; and administrative personnel and services must be in place to support institutional decisions. As the mission broadens and becomes more complex, so, too, do the requirements for budget planning at the institution.

This volume is not intended to be a budget primer. There are, however, certain basic budget principles that all planners must understand, inside and outside the budget office. We review these principles here briefly.

Revenue Streams

Depending upon the institution type, colleges and universities have multiple revenue streams, including (1) tuition and fees; (2) federal, state, and local government appropriations; (3) contracts, grants, and sponsored research; (4) gifts; (5) endowment support; and (6) auxiliary operations (functions not central to the education and general mission of the institution, e.g., dining services, residence halls, and bookstores).

Given the mission of the institution (including institutional control, i.e., public versus private), effective budget planning begins with an assessment of which revenue streams belong in the institutional mix and the relative contribution of each to the overall operating revenue of the institution.

It is important to remember that all revenue streams are not equal. Tuition is an unrestricted revenue stream that can be used as the institution sees fit within the operating budget. Contracts, grants, and sponsored research, while representing dollars flowing into the institution to support specific instructional, research, and public service activities, are restricted funds that can be spent only for the purpose for which they are designated. In negotiating contracts and grants, institutions are allowed to recover a portion of indirect costs, i.e., institutional costs that enable the research or service to take place on campus. Indirect costs include administrative services such as the accounts payable office processing payments associated with the contract or grant and institutional costs such as utilities. However, indirect cost recovery is certainly not a money-making revenue proposition (nor should it be). It is, at best, a break-even proposition and, more often than not, a loss leader among revenue streams.

Similarly, gifts are largely restricted at most institutions. While a college or university might like a multimillion dollar gift for general operations, the gift more often than not is specifically designated for general endowment, scholarship endowment, capital constriction, or some other specific-use category, and endowment funds may be similarly restricted. While the interest earned during a fiscal year from the general endowment is unrestricted and may be used for general operations, the corpus of funds that generates that interest is restricted and may not be drawn down except under legally specified circumstances.

The final category of revenues—auxiliary enterprises—is intended to be *at least* self-supporting and, in many instances, a source of income for the institution. With this basic understanding of revenue streams, a number of challenging issues confront budget planners:

- As tuition and fees constitute the largest revenue stream at most colleges and universities, a central issue is how tuition-dependent the institution should be. This is a critical concern at private institutions, where it is not uncommon for tuition to represent at least 80 to 90 percent of education and general revenues. (Education and general revenues represent those revenues that support the cost of doing business at a college or university—the core functions of teaching, research, and service and the activities that support them.) And it is becoming increasingly critical at public institutions, where declining state appropriations are placing more and more importance on tuition and fees as the primary revenue stream.

- If tuition is the revenue stream upon which an institution most heavily relies, what is institutional policy with respect to tuition discounting? While tuition may look robust on the revenue side of the balance sheet, to what extent is its true value being eroded by financial aid on the expenditure side? While student financial aid is frequently essential in attracting students to an institution, is there institutional consensus on the level of tuition discounting?

- Related to the previous point, where tuition is the central revenue stream, a crucial budget planning strategy is that of *pricing*. A significant number of students at any college or university *do not pay* the "sticker price," i.e., the schedule of tuition and fees that appears in the institution's catalog. Many students carry some measure of student aid that results in their paying a "net price." For the tuition revenue stream to cover its intended share of education and general expenditures, what does the institution's sticker price have to be in light of the net price that will likely be paid? This is not a simple arithmetic function. Sticker price has to be competitive with that of peer institutions and, from year-to-year, should be increased at a rate that is both representative of real increases in the cost of doing business at the institution and that is relatively predictable for the parents and students actually paying the price.

- It is bad fiscal policy to balance budgets continuously on the backs of students. Extraordinary external circumstances over which institutions have no control (such as significant reductions in state funding, economic recessions, and increases in the price of health insurance and utilities) do occur and force spikes in tuition rates. Therefore, it is important to diversify revenue streams to the greatest extent possible. Because contracts, grants, and sponsored research are not money makers, budget planners must consider other options. What is a reasonable target for a capital campaign to attract annual giving to support the institutional endowment? What pricing structures within auxiliary services provide the opportunity for more than self-support?

Until this point, we have looked only at revenue streams, which obviously get spent. We will focus next on expenditures.

Expenditure Categories

The major categories of expense that are found, to one extent or another, at most colleges and universities are (1) instruction; (2) academic support; (3) student services; (4) research and public service; (5) institutional support; (6) student aid; (7) mandatory transfers (including debt payments), other transfers, and changes in fund balances; and (8) auxiliary operations. Let us consider each of the expenditure categories and the issues that might be important to budget planners when examining expenses.

Instructional expenditures include the salaries of faculty and support personnel directly related to the teaching function. They also include instructional support costs—such as supplies, noncapital equipment, travel, and costs associated with instructional technology. In thinking about the level of instructional costs at the institution, budget planners might consider the following questions: Are faculty salaries and those of instructional support personnel sufficiently competitive to attract and retain those individuals most qualified and capable of realizing the teaching component of the instructional mission? Are benchmarking studies—including the American Association of University Professors faculty compensation survey , the College and University Professional Association for Human Resources (CUPA-HR) faculty salary surveys for four-year institutions and for community colleges, and the Oklahoma State

University Faculty Salary Survey being used to track salaries at the institutional and discipline level? Are the size of the academic department, magnitude of faculty teaching loads, and instructional costs at the academic discipline level being benchmarked with those at peer institutions and at aspirational institutions? Are personnel costs as a percentage of total instructional costs at the discipline level consistent with those at peer institutions?

Academic support expenses include salaries associated with academic administration (provosts, deans, and assistant and associate provosts and deans), library, and, where appropriate, academic computing. The same questions regarding faculty are relevant here, although the benchmarking tools are different. The CUPA-HR *Administrative Compensation Survey* (senior-level personnel), the CUPA-HR Mid-Level *Administrative & Professional Salary Survey*, and the *Association of Research Libraries Annual Salary Survey* are appropriate choices for monitoring salaries within the academic support area. Are staffing levels in academic support areas consistent with those at peer institutions and aspirational institutions? What sort of academic library is essential to support the institutional mission? To what extent is the library taking advantage of technology to reduce costs and enhance the delivery of library services?

Student services expenditures include the admissions and financial aid offices, registrar's office, counseling, and career services. Salary information for senior and mid-level student affairs personnel may be found in the same CUPA-HR sources cited above. Some professional organizations conduct their own salary surveys but do not broadly distribute the results. Unfortunately, there is very little beyond these sources in the way of consistent and reliable data in either student services or general institutional administrative areas. This underscores the importance of having a solid institutional research capability to support planning at a college or university. Institutional researchers can assist in defining appropriate peer groups and in constructing ad hoc survey instruments to collect needed staffing and cost data to inform student services expenditure decisions. That said, other factors deserve consideration. Is the institution taking full advantage of technology in delivering student services? For example, the University of Delaware was a national leader in establishing the concept of a one-stop student services facility where a student could register for courses, pay bills, sign up for meal plans, obtain a student identification card and/or parking permit, order transcripts, and perform other tasks, all without seeing more than one student services employee. By using Web-based technology, both within the student services facility and subsequently extended to the Internet, the university was able to reduce the number of personnel needed to deliver student services, the associated paperwork, and concomitant excess costs. A second area for consideration is whether selected student services can reasonably be moved to auxiliary, i.e., self-supporting, status. The University of Delaware made the determination in the mid-1990s to move certain student support services, e.g., student centers, to auxiliary service status, supported by mandatory student fees. While these services are not intended to make a profit, they are operating on a self-supporting business model that has enhanced their efficiency while in no way denigrating the level of services afforded students or student satisfaction with those services. Growing numbers of institutions across the United States are exploring this option.

As noted earlier, research and service expenditure levels are largely dictated by the contractor or grantor, and there is not a lot of latitude in that regard. However, data are available to address some components of this expenditure category. The magnitude and scope of extension activities can be benchmarked using data available from the National Association of State Universities and Land-Grant Colleges. Salaries of personnel in offices of sponsored research can be benchmarked using the CUPA-HR surveys, and institutional research can gather information on staffing patterns based upon total research/service expenditure volume. We should also point out that there is institutionally

funded research and service that falls under the rubric of departmental research. Paid for out of instructional funds, the magnitude of departmental research expenditures as a proportion of total instructional expense within a unit needs to be understood and periodically monitored.

Institutional support covers the costs of general administration and management of the institution. The salaries of most major senior and mid-level administrative positions can be benchmarked using the CUPA-HR salary surveys. Two major questions confront budget planners with respect to institutional support: Is the institution making maximum use of technology in delivering services? And are all of those services essential to the basic operating budget? Use of Web-based, distributed business applications— most notably through vendors such as Banner and Oracle-PeopleSoft—have enabled a number of institutions to move to virtually paperless environments and to substantially reduce both administrative personnel and associated costs. There are significant up-front costs in the selection, purchase, and installation of appropriate software and training, but over the long haul, institutional efficiency and cost-effectiveness are enhanced. With respect to the cost of institutional support services under the umbrella of the institution's basic operating budget, it is important to ask whether the service is essential to full realization of the institution's mission. Is food service in the dining halls integral to the mission of the institution, or can it be more efficiently and economically outsourced? The same question can be asked of a host of other services ranging from custodial operations to bookstores to publications production to pharmaceutical services. The questions may be answered differently from institution to institution, but the exercise of asking the questions is an important component of overall budget planning.

We noted earlier that what a college or university spends on financial aid directly affects both the net tuition price that students pay at the institution and the true level of tuition dependence at the school, both strategic considerations in budget planning. Garnering additional federal, state, and local aid dollars can help reduce the level of discounting as well as increase the level of endowed scholarships through fund-raising efforts.

Mandatory transfers include items such as debt service on buildings, and there is no avoiding them, other than to carry no debt at all. Other transfers are not mandatory, however, and are key components of institutional budget planning. For example, boards of trustees at many institutions mandate a policy that a certain percentage of revenues in a given year are to be set aside and invested as quasi-endowment. Those funds then become restricted, and only the interest on them can be used for operations in subsequent years. This is a forward-thinking mode of planning

intended to ensure the institution's future financial health.

It is important to remember that auxiliary services are essentially businesses to which best practices can and should be applied. The Council of Higher Education Management Associations is a consortium of groups focusing on management issues in higher education and embraces a number of organizations dedicated to best practices in auxiliary operations.

To conclude this brief overview of higher education revenue and expenditure concepts, we refer readers interested in learning more to the sources identified in the bibliography and list of resources found at the end of the volume. Finally, we should once again note the obvious cardinal rule of budget planning: *The level of recurring expenditures at a college or university must never exceed the level of recurring revenues.*

Having carefully considered the academic mission of the institution and the human and fiscal resources needed to support that mission, there is still need to plan for the physical resources to support that mission. For most colleges and universities, that translates into bricks and mortar—classroom and faculty office buildings, libraries, student services buildings, including residence and dining halls, and administrative support buildings. Additionally, it is increasingly important to include technology within the scope of physical services that deliver both traditional and nontraditional higher

education products. Chapter 5 focuses on
facilities planning in the broadest sense
of the term.

Chapter 5

Facilities/Physical Resources Planning

Thus far, we have described planning principles for the development of academic programs and services, and for stewardship of the human and fiscal resources to support those programs and services. But we have not addressed the physical environment. The vast majority of higher education institutions in the United States are not "virtual" colleges and universities; they require bricks and mortar—real facilities where programs and services can be delivered.

Facilities planning is far more than planning for the construction of a classroom building or a student center. It is the physical embodiment of the institution's mission. The campus facilities represent what an institution is about and how it hopes to interact with its various clientele groups. At the cornerstone of facilities planning is the campus master plan.

A campus master plan is not the vision of an architectural firm or facilities consultant. It is a carefully reasoned physical expression of a college's or university's mission. It is not a static document—i.e., once done, planning ceases. To the contrary, it is an ongoing process, subject to periodic reevaluation as demographic, economic, and political circumstances change and affect the campus. Facilities planning in general, and campus master planning in particular, is a collegial exercise. Most colleges and universities have facilities planning committees that typically involve members of the president's senior staff, facilities personnel, faculty and staff representatives, trustee representation, and occasionally student representatives. In developing or revising a campus master plan, the facilities planning committee must consider a number of fundamental questions:

- Is the institutional mission statement current? Since the scope of programs and services offered by a college or university is directly derived from the mission, it is important that the mission statement reflect what the institution is doing and what it intends to do in the foreseeable future. As noted earlier, mission statements are not arbitrary, but are rooted in the institution's traditions and values. That said, environmental circumstances do change over time, and some modification of mission is inevitable. The physical plant must ultimately reflect the institution's mission.

- Is the academic plan for the institution current, broadly understood, and representative of campus consensus? Specifically, does the plan address such issues as optimum student enrollment; optimum number of faculty; depth and breadth of curriculum; desired outcomes in the areas of teaching, research, and service; and available human and fiscal resources? The academic strategic plan at an institution drives—or should drive—the campus master plan and facilities planning. The academic plan specifies the extent to which the institution will grow (or in some instances, shrink), the teaching pedagogy and desired learning outcomes, academic and student support services to facilitate those outcomes, and the nature and scope of research and service activities. The physical plan should reflect these components of the academic plan, all of which are rooted in the institution's mission.

- Within the context of *existing* human and fiscal resources, what are institutional priorities with respect to facilities? What must be done within the next five years? In the five years thereafter?

In establishing institutional priorities, an important first step is assessing the extent to which *existing* facilities support the institution's mission and goals. Is capital construction an immediate necessity? Will the current physical plant—either in its current condition or in refurbished condition—be sufficient to satisfy the demands of the current academic plan? What are the required resources to sustain existing facilities and/or construct new facilities? In answering these questions, the facilities planning committee must consider several critical pieces of information. Does the academic plan call for changes in enrollment,

in the nature and scope of academic offerings, in the number of faculty, in the depth and breadth of research activity, in curriculum and pedagogy, or as the result of accreditation issues?

In addition, there are issues related to campus life that must be explored. Does the academic plan call for substantial changes in the depth and breadth of academic and student support services, in the on-campus residency policy for students, in the depth and breadth administrative and institutional services needed to support the academic plan, or in the depth and breadth of athletic and student recreation programs?

In responding to these questions from a facilities planning perspective, context is important. What is the current level of deferred maintenance on campus, and is addressing that issue more urgent than capital construction in addressing the overall facilities needs of the institution? What is the current level of operating budget support for physical plant operations and upkeep? Is it adequate, and does it allow for facilities renewal and renovation? Are the circumstances appropriate for launching a major capital campaign to support new construction? As these contextual questions are answered along with the basic academic questions that drive facilities planning, it is then possible to move forward with substantive master planning.

The starting point for master planning is not the campus itself, but the larger geographic region in which the campus is located. Are there major environmental issues or regulations that might affect construction and/or landscaping on campus? Are there changes in the immediate environs that might affect the campus? For example, is the Army Corps of Engineers about to dam a local river? Is the department of transportation bringing a major interstate highway adjacent to campus? Has the municipality in which the institution is located adopted ordinances that will hinder campus expansion? Have municipalities or state governments made voluntary commitments to measuring and reducing greenhouse gas emissions? These larger issues must be understood before focusing on campus planning.

Turning to the campus itself, it is important to start with the big picture. Within the context of existing facilities, what circulation patterns are optimally desirable for pedestrians, joggers, and bicycles? This helps determine placement of future classroom, laboratory, and academic or student support facilities. Similarly, what circulation patterns are optimally desirable for vehicles? This helps site parking lots and garages. In considering future construction, pragmatic and aesthetic judgments come into play. What is the topography of the campus? Not all soil types and terrains lend themselves to new construction. What are the campus's values with respect to natural and open space, green buildings, sustainable design, and renewable energy consumption? These values also affect

the site of a building. What is the impact of expansion on neighborhoods and on city/town services?

Before constructing a new building, a basic understanding of existing space is essential. Within current facilities, how much space does the institution actually have? How is it being used? Who is it assigned to, and what condition is it in? Is it appropriate space for the intended function? Reassigning space and/or renovating and refurbishing existing space may be more economical and efficient than new construction.

All campuses, whether a major research university with 30,000 students or a small regional community college with fewer than 2,500 students, should invest the necessary time and energy to construct an inventory of all of the facilities on campus. Such a tool is essential to exemplary facilities planning. A facilities inventory contains information on gross square footage and net assignable square footage for virtually all categories of space within a building (e.g., classroom, laboratory, office, study, general use, and special use) and within those categories the function of that space (e.g., instruction, research, public service, academic support, student support, and institutional support). Our purpose here is not to fully describe the components of a facilities inventory, but to make clear the importance of constructing such an inventory. A detailed description of the components of a facilities inventory appears in the National Center for Education Statistics publication *Postsecondary Education Facilities Inventory and Classification Manual* (FICM).[43]

Perhaps as important to facilities planners as having an accurate facilities inventory is the capability to benchmark institutional facilities data with that from similar institutions and institutions with facilities to which the focal campus aspires. The Campus Facilities Inventory (CFI) is an annual survey structured and predicated on the FICM. CFI is a valuable facilities planning tool that allows participating institutions to benchmark their own facilities data against that from other participating institutions. It can be accessed at www. scup.org/knowledge/cfi. The U.S. Energy Star Program (www.energystar.gov) helps benchmark energy consumption of facilities against similar campus buildings across the country.

Very few of us ever have the opportunity to plan a campus from scratch. The vast majority of facilities planners are working with a campus that is a patchwork quilt of old and new buildings, some of which will be serviceable for years so long as they are maintained, others whose useful life is fast drawing to a close. A number of basic principles should be the cornerstone of facilities planning on any campus. The first of these is minimizing

deferred maintenance. During difficult fiscal times, it is relatively easy and noncontroversial to avoid a major tuition hike, reduction in workforce, or other painful economic belt tightening by simply spending money that had been earmarked for operation and maintenance of the physical plant on other things. In our view, ongoing deferred maintenance, while occasionally unavoidable, is the physical manifestation of failure to plan in other areas of campus life.

To the extent possible, campuses should adhere to the following principle with respect to ongoing facilities maintenance. The lifespan of most buildings on a campus is generally acknowledged to be roughly fifty years. *If the institution annually allocates approximately 2 percent of the replacement value of the physical plant for facilities renewal and renovation, over the course of fifty years, sufficient funds will have been expended to fully sustain that physical plant.* A commitment of this sort is not trivial; it clearly implies full integration with academic and budget planning on campus to the point where decisions are made with respect to fiscal and human resource deployment that allow for the annual 2 percent allocation. A commitment of this nature indicates that the institution views the physical plant as a valuable asset that contributes in significant ways to the realization of the institution's mission and that it is an asset

43. National Center for Education Statistics, Postsecondary Education Facilities Inventory and Classification Manual, Washington, DC, www.nces.ed.gov/pubs92/92165.pdf.

to be preserved.

The sequencing of facilities renewal/renovation projects and/or new capital construction is generally a function of the overall master plan for the campus. Obviously, a natural disaster such as Hurricane Katrina, which struck several colleges and universities along the Gulf Coast in 2005; Hurricane Ivan, which struck the University of West Florida in 2004; or the Northridge earthquake, which struck California State University, Northridge in 1994, significantly alters such a master plan. These are exceptions, however; adherence to the master plan is generally the rule. And whether the project is renovation or new construction, certain specific planning questions require complete answers before moving forward:

- For what specific purposes will space within the building be used? Classroom instruction? Wet/dry laboratories? Offices? Compiling answers to such questions can be *facilitated* by either an external consultant or professionals within the campus's office of facilities planning and construction. The operative word is facilitated. The requirements for answering the question are part of the facilitation process, but the answers, in and of themselves, must ultimately come from the intended end-users of the facility and the space.

- What types of technology are required? What are the audiovisual requirements? Is the building to employ wireless LAN technology? What decisions should be made with respect to hazardous materials in laboratory spaces? The answers to these questions need to be very specific, as it is far easier—and less expensive—to introduce technology during the construction phase of a project than to introduce it once things are well under way.

- An emerging area of facilities planning that is receiving considerable attention is that of sustainability. What is the intended relationship, by virtue of design, between the facility and the environment? What opportunities exist for addressing conservation of natural resources, including energy and water? What is the intended relationship of open space/green space to building design? What should designers consider to take advantage of conservation opportunities, energy management, pollution reduction, alternative fuel fleets, sustainable living residence halls, and effective recycling, to name a few possibilities. Increasingly, colleges and universities are using a planning and design process that includes life cycle analyses of the environmental, social, and economic impacts of the facilities and operations.

- What are the campus aesthetics, and how should this project design be consistent with that aesthetic?

This, too, is not a trivial question. Campuses such as the University of Virginia and the University of Delaware pride themselves on the consistent architectural design of central campus buildings. Other state-related institutions are more concerned with the cost of the project and have multiple architectural styles on campus. The aesthetic values for the institution must be clearly articulated before the first shovel of dirt is dug from the ground.

- Which consultant, architect, contractor, and construction manager can best bring this project to fruition in the time frame, style, quality, and cost of construction that has been stipulated? Some institutions are mandated by law to accept low-bid proposals for work. However, in our view, it is more important to look at the body of work of the individual involved in the proposal to ensure that it is consistent—particularly with respect to quality and cost efficiency—with the intended outcome for this project. In simply choosing the low bid, the total cost of the project may be far more than anticipated. The Association for the Advancement of Sustainability in Higher Education (www.aashe.org) has policy banks that include sample design and operational policies to help institutions avoid the pitfalls of the low bid.

This discussion is intended to give you an overview of the general principles of good facilities planning. Those seeking greater depth and breadth of knowledge with respect to facilities planning should consult the sources identified in the bibliography and resources section found at the conclusion of this volume.

Chapter 6

Understanding the Language of Planning

As a campus contemplates how best to move forward with academic, resource, and facilities planning, it is important to remember that these are not planning silos that operate independently and isolated from each other. Academic planning provides a framework within which resource and facilities planning occurs. All three types of planning are interrelated, and effective integration of these processes is essential to moving the institution forward.

Planning at a college or university is grounded in the institution's mission. As we discussed in chapter 3, a mission statement is a carefully reasoned statement that describes what an institution wishes to be and what it values. From that mission statement, planning goals are derived that provide general policy direction

for the institution. And those planning goals, in turn, should lend themselves to *measurable* planning objectives that guide assessment of institutional progress in meeting those planning goals.

Consider the University of Delaware's mission statement, cited in chapter 3. Certainly, the university's mission statement is not appropriate for every institution of higher education. But for that specific institution, it gives a clear sense of the type of student it strives to attract; the balance between undergraduate and graduate instruction; the extent of the role that the university wishes to play in engaging in pure and applied research; and public service as manifested in its land grant, sea grant, space grant, and urban grant designations. While this mission and values set may not be applicable to all institutions, what is portable is the need

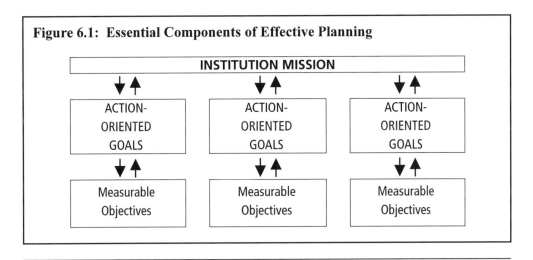

Figure 6.1: Essential Components of Effective Planning

INSTITUTION MISSION

| ACTION-ORIENTED GOALS | ACTION-ORIENTED GOALS | ACTION-ORIENTED GOALS |

| Measurable Objectives | Measurable Objectives | Measurable Objectives |

for clarity in what an institution wishes to be and the educational, cultural, and social values that it considers to be at its core.

A clearly articulated mission statement provides a basis for developing action-oriented goal statements and measurable planning objectives. Figure 6.1 illustrates this concept. Goal statements derived from the mission help define institutional policy. For example, a portion of the University of Delaware's mission statement indicates that "The University reaffirms its historic mission to provide the highest quality education for its undergraduate students." Such a statement underscores the primacy of undergraduate instruction in the curriculum and provides a clear direction for planning activity. The question for planners is how, precisely, to provide that high-quality undergraduate instruction.

The "how" translates into specific, action-oriented planning goals aimed at moving the institution toward a fuller realization of its mission. A goal related to that undergraduate education mission statement might be: "The University will continue to attract and retain the most academically talented and diverse undergraduate students, and support their intellectual, cultural, and ethical development as citizens, scholars, and professionals." In addition, just as goal statements are derived from the institution's mission, the extent to which they are achieved feeds back into the realization of that mission. Hence, figure

6.1 has two-way arrows between mission and goals.

Note that the goal statement above contains action verbs such as "attract," "retain," and "support." The action verbs in goal statements need to be translated into measurable planning objectives that enable an assessment of the extent to which planning goals are achieved. Consider the following planning objectives as they relate to attracting, retaining, and academically supporting undergraduate students at the institution:

1. Retain a freshman admissions target of 3,200 to 3,400 students annually, with an admissions profile for academic year 2007 of 23,000 applications, a 40 percent admit rate, and a yield rate in excess of 35 percent.

2. Improve the alignment of undergraduate enrollment distribution and instructional resource distribution across the disciplines, especially with respect to faculty.

3. Review and revise undeclared student status with respect to academic major through improved matching of students and majors upon admission, improved early advisement for new students, creation of "college" majors, and establishment of a university studies option.

4. Maintain a freshman-to-sophomore retention rate above the national average for highly selective institutions, and seek to achieve a consistent rate of 90 percent or higher.

5. Maintain a graduation rate above the national average for highly selective institutions, and seek to achieve a six-year rate of 75 percent or higher.

6. Increase minority and international enrollment, with retention and graduation rates for those populations consistent with university-wide averages for all students.[44]

The first objective relates to attracting and retaining students. Lower admit rates enable greater selectivity within the applicant pool, while higher yield rates mean that more high-quality admitted students actually attend. The stipulation of specific target admit and yield rates provides a benchmark against which enhanced admissions activity can be measured.

The second and third objectives relate to supporting academic success for admitted students. Allocating faculty lines to academic programs consistent with levels of student subscription ensures that students will be able to get courses in timely manner for steady progress to graduation, although achieving this end may be complicated and difficult to achieve for a number of reasons. Similarly, appropriate academic advising that matches academic majors with students' academic skills and strengths increases the likelihood of student success. Objectives 4 and 5 stipulate specific retention and graduation rates for the overall student body, while objective 6 indicates that increased enrollments among underrepresented and international students should reflect retention and graduation rates consistent with the total student body.

An essential and defining characteristic of good planning is that it is measurable. Colleges and universities embarking on any planning process, be it long range, strategic, or tactical (we will discuss the differences shortly), require a systematic institutional research capability. While smaller institutions may not have an office of institutional research, per se, they must nonetheless have the capability of quantitatively and qualitatively assessing the extent to which planning objectives are being achieved, planning goals are moving forward, and the institution's mission is being realized.

Like the relationship between mission and goals in figure 6.1, the relationship between goals and objectives is characterized by two-way arrows. Goals give rise to objectives, and to the extent that those objectives are measurably achieved, goals may become more fully realized or modified.

While not requiring the broad consensus of a campus mission statement, planning goals and objectives are nonetheless collaborative. They are not the edicts of the provost's office or some other

44. University of Delaware, "Report to the Faculty Senate: Academic Progress at the University of Delaware," February 2005, Newark, DE, www.udel.edu/provost/AcademicProgress.pdf.

administrative epicenter. The definition of planning goals and concomitant measurable objectives are typically the product of specific campus working groups familiar with the specific planning area. For example, appropriate retention and graduation goals and objectives are the product of extended conversations between the admissions office, the academic administration, the faculty, and, where available and appropriate, the office of institutional research.

It must be underscored that the foregoing planning examples are rooted in the institutional culture of the University of Delaware and are not universally applicable to all higher education institutions. However, the planning constructs and principles that underpin those examples are, indeed, portable across institutions. Where the faculty and staff at the University of Delaware have, within the context of their institutional mission, defined a highly selective undergraduate admissions process that ultimately yields graduation rates significantly above the norm for four-year public institutions, other colleges and universities make different choices that are appropriate to their individual circumstances.

With a basic understanding of the interrelationships between institutional mission, planning goals, and measurable objectives, let us now move the discussion to a more concrete set of issues that help to define the academic planning process.

Strategic, Long-Range, Tactical, and Operational Plans

The terms "strategic," "long-range," "tactical," and "operational" are often used as labels for different types of planning. Long-range, tactical, and operational planning labels are usually used to distinguish among a variety of plans that address different time horizons.

Long-range plans are those that address how the institution will fulfill its mission. Long-range planning at a college or university is a comprehensive process, integrating and synthesizing a broad range of planning goals and objectives that are derived from the overarching umbrella of the institution's mission. It is not unusual for the campus plan to be an extensive document, with goals and objectives grouped under such headings as Academic Support Services, Administration, Admissions, Faculty, Finances, Governance, Physical Plant and Equipment, Program and Curriculum, Research and Public Service, and Student Services. Traditionally, a ten-year time frame might have been attached to such plans. However, given the nature and speed of change in today's environment, some believe that the appropriate time frame for a long-range plan should probably be in the five- to seven-year range.

Tactical plans are those that translate long-range goals into intermediate priorities. Time frames may extend to the range of three years, and there are usually explicit linkages to regular decision-making and budgeting processes. An operational plan generally defines activities that will be addressed within a year and incorporated in an annual budget process.

Strategic planning refers to the setting of priorities for addressing matters of critical importance to the institution, regardless of the planning time frame. Donald Norris and Nick Poulton cite Robert Shirley's criteria for identifying strategic issues as those that:

- Define the institution's relationship to its environment

- Generally take the whole organization as the unit of analysis

- Depend on inputs from a variety of functional areas

- Provide direction for, and constraints on, administrative and operational activities throughout the institution.[45]

An example may serve to illustrate the difference between strategic planning and plans that focus on a specific time frame. As important as long-range planning is in setting a comprehensive direction for institutional decisions and resource allocations, the very magnitude of the long-range plan is limiting. Put quite simply, there are not enough resources at any one time to achieve all of the goals and objectives that are typically articulated in a long-range

plan. Institutions are forced to prioritize those goals and objectives that are of immediate importance and to allocate resources accordingly. In other words, they must think and behave *strategically*.

Institutional and Unit Planning; Centralized and Decentralized Planning

At first glance, the terms "institutional and unit planning" and "centralized and decentralized planning" may appear to refer to the same thing. There are, however, two different concepts which require explanation. First, the idea of institutional versus unit planning can be employed to describe activity that takes place at different organizational levels. The most highly publicized planning activities are frequently those that take place at the institutional level. However, it is also important that planning occur at the academic and administrative unit levels and that those sets of activities are actively linked to the institutional plan to provide some assurance that everyone is moving forward, down the same road, together.

The terms "centralized" and "decentralized" planning may be used to refer to differences in decision-making philosophy and execution, as the following example illustrates. The question as to whether centralized or decentralized planning is preferable is largely a function of the organizational culture at a college or university. For

45. Donald M. Norris and Nick L. Poulton, *A Guide for New Planners*, 1991 ed. (Ann Arbor, MI: Society for College and University Planning, 1991), 8.

example, in the late 1980s and early 1990s, when the University of Delaware endured a succession of presidents and severe budget constraints, planning was largely centralized. Reestablishing a budget with recurring expenditures funded from recurring revenue sources required close oversight at senior levels of the administration. The university utilized a central Budget Council that was co-chaired by the provost and executive vice president, with representative deans and department chairs, and staff support from the university budget director, the assistant provost for academic budget planning, and the assistant vice president for institutional research and planning. The Budget Council met with academic deans and administrative vice presidents to review planning initiatives and oversee allocation of resources. Because new monies were scarce to nonexistent, funding decisions entailed reallocation of existing human and fiscal resources in a manner consistent with the mission of the institution. The metrics and ground rules that supported resource reallocation decisions were broadly publicized and understood. While those decisions may not have been universally embraced, the need for a focused linkage between planning and budgeting was broadly supported.

Ten years later, the stability of senior administration and the economic environment in which the university operated had improved by orders of magnitude. Budgeting and planning at

the university moved from a centralized to a decentralized mode of operation, and the university now utilizes a block budget methodology wherein the president, provost, and executive vice president divide the operating budget into academic, administrative, and general institutional blocks of funds. The provost and executive vice president then further allocate those blocks of funds to each of the university's colleges and major administrative units (e.g., human resources, information technology, and facilities planning and construction). Each of these units is then charged with responsibility for managing those funds in a fashion consistent with the institutional mission. For example, the College of Arts and Sciences receives its annual block of operating funds with the understanding that it is free to use those resources to fund new planning initiatives, but with the further understanding that there will be no additional resources over and above the allocated block. Consequently, the college is responsible for making the same sort of resource allocation and reallocation decisions for its departments and programs that were made centrally by the Budget Council a decade earlier.

It is not uncommon at colleges and universities to find planning processes that are hybrids of centralized and decentralized planning. Facilities planning is frequently just such a hybrid. When designing a classroom building, for example, planning is only as participatory as it has to be, involving faculty from those departments affected and characterized by centralized budget control intended to prevent or minimize cost overruns. Planning for an institution-wide capital campaign is similarly hybrid—there is generally no institution-wide committee establishing campaign targets or determining how to invest gift funds resulting from the campaign. Participation in campaign planning is usually targeted—public relations personnel to publicize the campaign, development office personnel to pursue core donors, perhaps a dean or two from professional schools to target corporate donors, and investment personnel to determine how best to grow the endowment.

Whether constructing a new classroom building or attempting to expand gifts to an institution, the mission of a college or university is the context against which planning processes are implemented. Colleges and universities tend to build facilities consistent with their mission; for example, Amherst College has no agricultural experiment station, and most community colleges have no residence hall complex.

The intent of this chapter was to acquaint you with the terminology commonly used in discussions about planning. While the relationship between and among mission, goals, and objectives is important, as are the distinctions between long-range, strategic, and tactical planning, the most important aspect of planning is simply to plan.

If an institution is to invest significant time in any aspect of planning, clarity of mission should be at the top of the list of priorities. Policy-oriented goals and measurable objectives are relatively meaningless unless an institution has a clear sense of what it wishes to be, the values that it embraces, and its relationships with internal and external constituencies. Without a clear sense of mission, planning—such as it is—reflects environmental trends and current internal institutional circumstances, hardly a recipe for longevity and viability. On the other hand, a clear sense of mission provides a rich template within which policy-oriented goals and measurable objectives can be articulated and within which strategic and tactical decisions can be made.

Chapter 7

Strategies for Assessing Results

Our discussion thus far has focused on planning processes. For those processes to work effectively, they must be informed with reliable information. An institution must be able to assess where it is to plan where it wants to go. These assessments refer not only to how effectively and efficiently a college or university operates. Equally important is assessment of how and how much students learn during their years of study.

Assessments should not represent merely institutional responses to external demands for accountability. However, if done correctly, assessments certainly can serve that end. Quantitative and qualitative information about all facets of a college or university's operations—and how they relate to the institutional mission—is absolutely essential to good planning. This chapter contains a discussion of strategies that can be employed in assessing various aspects of institutional and educational effectiveness. Under the institutional effectiveness heading, we explore methods for assessing academic progress, budget/financial progress, and facilities/physical resources progress. Under the heading of educational effectiveness, we consider methods for assessing the student experience, academic program review, and student learning outcomes.

The focus of assessments should be both external and internal. In most instances, an institution should be able to benchmark its progress against comparable institutions or available norms. It should also view its progress in the context of internal history (for example, through the use of trend data).

Environmental scanning has become something of a cliché in higher education, but it is imperative that an institution be able to describe its position quantitatively and qualitatively within the current higher education marketplace and describe changes in that marketplace that may affect that position. Within the context of that environmental data, the institution charts its direction; in other words, it plans.

This chapter focuses on the components of effective analyses and assessments in support of planning and illustrates those components with specific examples. In some institutions, an office of institutional research may be the locus for most assessment-oriented work. However, some important aspects of assessment work may be housed in various locations depending on the organizational history and culture of a specific campus. The capacity to create and maintain institutional research

Figure 7.1: Analytical Research Projects Supporting Assessment of Institutional Effectiveness

Development and implementation of an assessment process that evaluates effectiveness in the following component areas: (1) achieving mission and goals; (2) implementing planning, resource allocation, and institutional renewal processes; (3) using institutional resources efficiently; (4) providing leadership and governance; (5) providing administrative structures and services; (6) demonstrating institutional integrity; and (7) assuring that institutional processes and resources support appropriate learning and other outcomes for students and graduates.

Assessment Tool	Primary Measure	Secondary Measure	Tertiary Measure
Academic Program Review Data	1	2	3
Economic Impact Analysis	1	---	---
Budget Support Notebooks	2	3	---
Campus Climate Survey	2	4	6
College Student Selection Survey (ASQ)	2	7	6
Delaware Study of Instructional Costs and Productivity	2	3	---
Enrollment Projection Model	2	---	---
Financial Aid Yield Model	2	3	---
Persisters Analysis	2	7	---
Salary Benchmarking Studies	2	3	6
Salary Equity Studies	2	3	6
State Budget Development Support	3	2	1
Employee Satisfaction Survey	4	3	6
ACT Survey of Student Opinions	5	2	7
Affirmative Action Analyses	6	2	1
Commission on Status of Women Analyses	6	2	1
ACT Student Needs Assessment Survey	7	2	---
Alumni Survey	7	2	---
Career Plans Survey	7	1	---
Grade Distribution Analysis	7	6	---
Induced Courseload Matrix	7	2	---
National Survey of Student Engagement	7	2	---
NCAA Compliance Analyses	7	6	2
ACT Survey of Academic Advising	2	7	---
Affirming Academic Priorities	1	7	---
Internal Audit/Budget Control	3	2	---
Space Utilization Studies			
Professional Accreditation Self-Study Analyses	7	2	1
Assessment of Student Learning	7	2	1

in support of planning is much more important than the organizational structure employed.

Institutional Effectiveness Assessments

Assessing Academic Progress

What sorts of quantitative and qualitative measurement strategies should be basic to an understanding of institutional effectiveness? It is once again useful to turn to a regional accrediting body to provide context for answering that question.

The Middle States Commission on Higher Education's accreditation criteria includes Standard 7, which is devoted to assessment of institutional effectiveness. This standard requires that an institution develop and implement an assessment process that evaluates its overall effectiveness in achieving its mission and goals and its compliance with accreditation standards. Comparable emphasis on assessing institutional effectiveness is found in the accreditation standards in each of the other regional accrediting bodies in the United States.

Institutional effectiveness is the perfect umbrella for assessing planning activity at an institution. If planning is well thought out and effectively executed, the institution should be "effective" in realizing its mission. Middle States Standard 7 can be broken down into subcomponents for analytical purposes. Specifically, in looking at the issue of institutional effectiveness, one might wish to assess the extent to which an

institution is achieving its mission and goals; implementing planning, resource allocation, and institutional renewal processes; using institutional resources effectively; providing leadership and governance; providing administrative structures and services; demonstrating institutional integrity; and assuring that institutional processes and resources support appropriate learning and other outcomes for its students and graduates. Figure 7.1 displays a nonexhaustive matrix of analytical projects that might well comprise a reasonable program of institutional research directed at assessing institutional effectiveness. Activities under scrutiny fall under the domains of academic planning, human resources planning, budget planning, and facilities planning.

A discussion of the major components of assessment activity in functional areas follows. It will become clear from the discussion that, while institutions need not have a formal office of institutional research, the scope of research activity should be sufficiently comprehensive that it makes good sense to staff for it appropriately. The numbers under the primary, secondary, and tertiary measure columns refer to the seven elements embedded in the language of the standard.

Most colleges and universities have missions that revolve around the cornerstone activities of teaching, research, and service. Multiple measures help to assess the extent to which the institution is fulfilling those mission functions. For example, the teaching function is addressed directly through the assessment of student learning, which we will discuss later in this chapter. But the teaching function is addressed through other measures as well. Many institutions have a systematic process of academic program review wherein academic units engage in self-study directed at producing a document for review by a panel of internal and sometimes external faculty/experts who are distinguished in the discipline. An institutional research capability provides data that are essential to program review that include the following:

- Trends in student credit hour production and average class size

- Trends in departmental student credit hour consumption by home major and by majors from other departments

- Grade distribution analyses

- Trends in department majors and minors

- Postgraduation activity of department majors

- Trends in departmental staffing patterns

- Trends in departmental revenue, by source

- Trends in departmental expenditures, by object and function

Academic program reviews are designed to evaluate the quality, productivity, and role of each academic unit and program in the fulfillment of the institution's mission and strategic goals. Program reviews serve to encourage ongoing self-study and planning within units, ensure comparability among review reports, and strengthen the linkages connecting the planning agendas and practices of individual units with those of the institution as a whole. Program reviews should inform budgetary planning decisions at every level of administration.

Student evaluation of instruction is another view of teaching effectiveness. A number of commercial vendors provide both hard-copy and Web-based instruments for assessing student satisfaction with instruction in individual courses. The IDEA Student Ratings of Instruction, housed at Kansas State University, is among the more prominent instruments nationally, and other vendors can be identified through a simple Web search. Alternatively, an increasing number of colleges and universities are opting to create their own Web-based instruments to ensure interdepartmental comparability that addresses the specific instructional objectives of the institution.

A number of indirect measures and evaluate the effectiveness of instructional activity. The institutional research program should include regular monitoring of persistence and graduation rates for all students. The fact that a proportion of students persists from year to year and another proportion ultimately graduates is not evidence, in and of itself, of instructional effectiveness. Persistence and graduation rates should be examined in conjunction with student satisfaction scores on a variety of measures, including quality of instruction in the academic major, quality of academic advising, and availability of instructors and advisors. These measures, in turn, are coupled with other assessments, including the proportion of graduates who obtain full-time employment, both within and outside the major field of study, and those who go on to pursue graduate study, with special attention to the schools where they are accepted. All that said, the most important measures of teaching effectiveness are those related to assessments of student learning outcomes; we will discuss those strategies shortly.

Institutional research can be of enormous value in planning for the allocation and use of academic resources, both human and fiscal, within a college or university. The decision to assign additional dollars and faculty lines to a department or program should be rooted in some relative measure of cost-effectiveness and productivity. And since most such decisions are a function of resource reallocation as opposed to the allocation of new resources, the same sorts of cost and productivity measures should provide an empirical basis for determining from where those resources will be reallocated.

An example of how institutional

research can effectively marry teaching load and fiscal data for support of budget decisions includes the budget support data described in chapter nine of this volume. Budget support data enable appropriate interdepartmental comparisons within a college or university, e.g. physics with chemistry, philosophy with English, art with music. An even more useful planning tool is one that enables a provost, dean, or department chair to compare selected budget support metrics with other departments at peer institutions and at institutions with reputations to which departments aspire. In other words, a source for national benchmarking of teaching loads and instructional costs is useful. The following pages describe just such a benchmarking capability. We want to stress that, wherever obtainable, benchmarking data such as this may give planners essential context for charting institutional directions.

In 1992, the University of Delaware's Office of Institutional Research and Planning initiated the Delaware Study of Instructional Costs and Productivity,[46] which has grown into a national data-sharing consortium embracing nearly 400 four-year colleges and universities, sharing detailed information on teaching loads, instructional costs, and externally funded scholarship. Figure 7.2 is a snapshot of the Delaware Study data that are provided annually. The focus is on tenured and tenure-track faculty

46. University of Delaware, "Delaware Study of Instructional Costs and Productivity." Newark, DE, www.udel.edu/ir/cost.

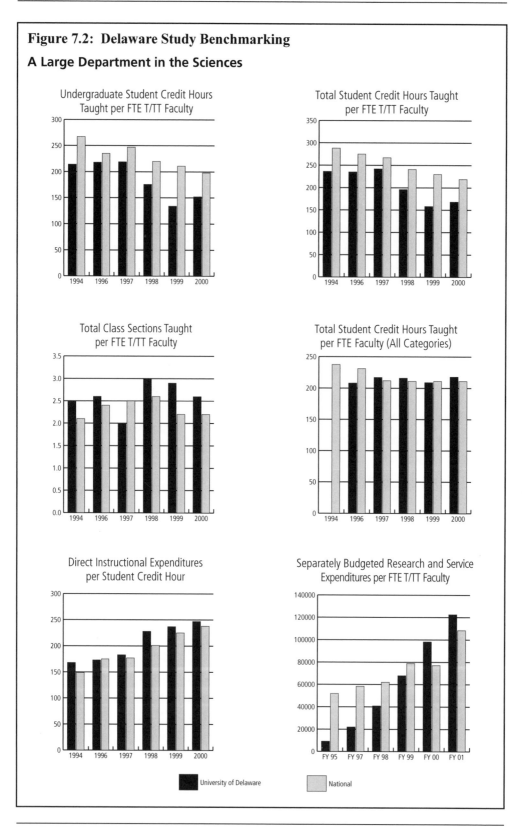

Figure 7.2: Delaware Study Benchmarking

A Large Department in the Sciences

(although the charts could be replicated for full-time nontenurable faculty, supplemental/adjunct faculty, or graduate teaching assistants) and examines the following variables over a five-year time frame, comparing University of Delaware measures with the national benchmark for research universities participating in the Delaware Study:

- Undergraduate student credit hours taught/full-time-equivalent (FTE) faculty

- Total student credit hours taught/FTE faculty

- Total academic year student credit hours/FTE faculty (all categories)

- Organized class sections taught/FTE faculty

- Direct instructional expense/student credit hour taught

- Research/services expenditures per FTE faculty

The data are presented to departments as a tool of inquiry as to why university departmental measures are similar to or different from national benchmark scores. The research university benchmark is the first cut at comparisons. It is possible to refine benchmarks further into specific peer groups that are defined by various end users—a provost, a dean, or a department chair, for example. Departments at the University of Delaware typically ask the Office of Institutional Research and Planning to do peer studies involving selected subsets of institutions participating in the Delaware Study in any given year. Thus, instead of being wedded to a benchmark that embraces all research institutions, the Department of History can select a peer group appropriate to that discipline, while the Department of Chemistry and Biochemistry can select an entirely different peer group.

Deans and department chairs make various uses of Delaware Study data in their academic planning. In instances where the study's output data, as measured in terms of student credit hours taught, is significantly above the national benchmark for tenured and tenure-track faculty, the case can be made for additional faculty lines. Figure 7.2 illustrates another use of Delaware Study data in conversations between a provost and a department chair. As is evident, in 1994 and 1996 (and prior years, for that matter), the volume of teaching activity by tenured and tenure-track faculty in this particular department approached the national benchmark for research universities. On the other hand, externally funded scholarship in those years was barely on the radar screen when compared with the national benchmark. In discussing this with the new department chair in 1996, the provost agreed to a reduction in teaching activity to allow tenured and tenure-track faculty more time to prepare grant proposals and, when funded, to engage in the actual research. As figure 7.2 clearly demonstrates, this planning initiative produced the desired end.

Two-year colleges have access to a benchmarking study comparable to the Delaware Study. Johnson County Community College is home to the Kansas Study, a national study of community college instructional costs and productivity supported by the Fund for the Improvement of Postsecondary Education (FIPSE). The Kansas Study, like the Delaware Study, collects data on teaching loads and instructional costs at the academic discipline level of analysis. However, the Kansas Study is sensitive to the different structure of disciplines within two-year institutions. It has structured a discipline taxonomy that is based upon Classification of Instructional Programs codes but that reflects those differences in a fashion that allows institutions to report data in a consistent fashion across institutional boundaries. Similarly, the Kansas Study addresses the different funding mechanisms from four-year institutions that underpin instructional expenditures. Interested readers can learn more about the Kansas Study at www.kansasstudy.org.

As useful as certain types of benchmarks data can be in academic planning, it is important to recognize and acknowledge limitations in those data. While measures such as student credit hours taught per FTE faculty or direct instructional expense per student credit hour taught are extremely useful in academic planning, neither measure captures the qualitative dimension of departmental activity. The Delaware Study is currently expanding under a grant from FIPSE

to collect benchmark data on selected measures of out-of-classroom faculty activity, including teaching support activity (such as advising, dissertation/ thesis work, and curriculum design), scholarship (such as publication, contract and grant activity, and professional development), and service (public service, institutional service, and service to the profession). The intention is to make benchmark information available on these measures, again at the academic discipline level of analysis, to provide context for looking at teaching loads and instructional costs and to describe more fully what faculty do, highlighting the differences between and among disciplines.

Other types of benchmark data are readily available to assist institutions in identifying their position in the higher education universe and in charting a future course. For example, for an institution to attract and retain the most talented faculty and professional and salaried staff, compensation levels must be competitive. In determining where the institution stands with respect to compensation, it is important to establish an appropriate comparator group and to do so in collaboration with affected constituencies. As an example, the University of Delaware is a collective bargaining campus with respect to faculty, and the Office of Institutional Research and Planning worked with the campus chapter of the American Association of University Professors (AAUP) in defining the peer group.

For cost-of-living comparisons, the University of Delaware's peer group was defined as Category I doctoral universities, identified annually in the AAUP magazine, *Academe*, in the states contiguous to Delaware and the District of Columbia. The March–April 2005 issue of *Academe*, titled "The Annual Report on the Economic Status of the Profession," reports average salary and total compensation (salary plus benefits) by rank (full, associate, and assistant professor; instructor; and lecturer) for nearly 1,500 colleges and universities across the United States. Because *Academe* includes a broad range of postsecondary institutions in its annual compensation issue, it is relatively easy for comprehensive, baccalaureate, and two-year institutions to similarly establish appropriate peer groups.

As important as it is to have general information on average salary and total compensation by institution, it is also important to have average salary data by academic discipline. Oklahoma State University conducts an annual salary study of member institutions of the National Association of State Universities and Land-Grant Colleges (NASULGC). The study reports average salary, by rank, for all academic disciplines at participating institutions and also reports average salary for new assistant professors, an important piece of data in ensuring market-competitive salary offers. Comparable data for non-NASULGC institutions is available from the College and University Professional

Association for Human Resources (CUPA-HR) as part of its annual study of faculty salaries. CUPA-HR also provides average salary data for senior and mid-level professional administrative personnel, data that are exceptionally useful in ensuring that compensation is competitive.

An important strategic planning concept, in addition to competitive compensation, is equitable compensation for employees. Institutional research offices frequently are asked to conduct salary equity analyses. The methodology applies multiple regression analysis to standard quantifiable demographic variables (e.g., rank, years in rank, and years at the university) to identify instances of potential salary inequities. These findings are then shared with deans and department chairs to determine if the apparent inequities are real or can be explained as a function of job performance. Salary compression and inversion are more likely problems with professional staff, and institutional research can provide analysis in these instances as well.

Assessing Budget/Financial Progress

In chapter 4, we discussed the various categories of institutional revenues and expenditures, and how they fit into the overall process of budget planning. But how does one assess the effectiveness of that budget planning, i.e., performance? In our experience, it is often difficult to sustain the attention not only of faculty, but of many administrators when discussing financial analyses. Yet these analyses can be critical to sustaining institutional vitality and viability.

An important starting point in framing *usable* financial assessments is to determine precisely what question the assessment should answer. We know that most academic units at an institution engage in teaching and that certain costs are associated with that activity. A unit's instructional budget is comprised of a number of expenditure categories, but by far the largest (85 to 90 percent at most institutions) is faculty salaries. To what extent does the teaching done by faculty generate tuition revenue in sufficient quantity to offset instructional costs? This is not a trivial question, but one that goes to the heart of an institution's mission. Beyond teaching, if departments or programs are expected to engage, in varying degrees, in research and service, are appropriate economies in place to sustain all of these activities?

It is best when doing financial assessments to keep the discussion as simple as possible. For example, when discussing instructional expenditures with noneconomists, the focus probably should be on *direct* instructional expense. The National Center for Education Statistics, through the Integrated Postsecondary Education Data System (IPEDS) Finance Survey, has developed a series of definitions with respect to what constitutes direct expense in a

series of functional areas at any college or university—e.g., instruction, academic support, student services, institutional support, research, and service. The definition for instructional expense is as follows:

> Expenses of the colleges, schools, departments, and other instructional divisions of the institution and expenses for departmental research and public service that are not separately budgeted should be included in this classification. Include expenses for both credit and noncredit activities. Exclude expenses for academic administration where the primary function is administration (e.g., academic deans). . . The instruction category includes academic instruction, occupational and vocational instruction, community education, preparatory and adult basic education, and remedial and tutorial instruction conducted by the teaching faculty for the institution's students.[47]

The wisdom of describing instructional costs in terms of direct expenses should be readily apparent. There is consistency and clarity across departments and disciplines with respect to what gets counted as an expense. Moving into indirect costs quickly muddies that consistency and clarity. Does a doctorate-granting chemical engineering department get charged more of the cost of the office of graduate studies than the baccalaureate-only anthropology department? Does the

---

47. National Center for Education Statistics, Integrated Postsecondary Education Data System (IPEDS) Finance Survey, nces.ed.gov/ipeds/pdf/Webbase2000/f1a_inst.pdf, 9-10.

physics department get charged a larger share of the office of contracts and grants than the art department? How does one charge back undergraduate admissions to academic departments—on the basis of a declared major that may change several times before graduation? Constructing a formula that sensibly assesses indirect cost is difficult enough; getting diverse audiences to understand it and achieve consensus is daunting.

Let's examine a real-world academic department. The Department of History at the University of Delaware taught a total of 21,640 student credit hours during the 2003–04 fall and spring terms, the terms that are funded by the basic instructional budget. The department's instructional budget for that year was $3,342,790. How much of that was covered by department teaching activity? Remembering that this is not an exercise in accounting, but a financial assessment to be understood by noneconomists and nonaccountants, revenue from teaching was calculated as follows: total tuition revenue at the university for basic instructional budget units was $198,696,190. This was divided by the total number of student credit hours taught in fall 2003 and spring 2004, i.e., 465,670, to arrive at a "per credit hour revenue unit" of $427. The $427 revenue unit was then multiplied by the 21,640 student credit hours taught by History faculty to arrive at $9,240,280 "earned income from instruction." If we then move to an income-to-expense ratio, where the $9,240,280 earned

income is divided by the $3,342,790 direct instructional expense incurred by History, the resulting quotient is 2.76. This suggests that the department generates from teaching activity nearly three times in revenue what it costs to deliver that instruction. Keep in mind that these are direct expenses and do not represent a full costs analysis, but they are nonetheless useful when making cross-departmental comparisons.

The comparable income-to-expense ratio for the Department of Chemical Engineering in 2003–04 was 0.37, and for the Department of Plant and Soil Sciences it was 0.05, suggesting that neither is covering its direct instructional expense with revenue from teaching activity. However, both departments are equipment-intensive science programs that have substantial numbers of small-group laboratories and primarily service their own majors. History, on the other hand, largely utilizes traditional lecture pedagogy, is uninhibited by equipment constraints, and services substantial numbers of nonmajors to meet general education requirements. Looking at the triad components of the university mission, teaching, research, and service, History quantitatively excels in teaching, while Chemical Engineering and Plant and Soil Sciences quantitatively excel in research. In fiscal year 2004, externally funded research and service expenditures per FTE tenured and tenure-track faculty in Chemical Engineering totaled $326,830, while those in Plant and Soil Sciences were $156,150 and those in

History were $1,000 per FTE tenured and tenure-track faculty member.

While this financial assessment is particularly useful for determining the extent to which academic departments cover their instructional costs through teaching activity, it is also a useful teaching tool in and of itself. Making cross-departmental comparisons such as those among History, Chemical Engineering, and Plant and Soil Sciences at the University of Delaware has helped underscore for the faculty and other constituencies the nature of mission at that institution. The data underscore that the University of Delaware is a *uni*versity—one institution with a three-faceted mission of teaching, research, and service, not a loose confederation of fifty-six fiefdoms/departments, each operating independently of one another. Where one department contributes significantly to the teaching portion of the university mission, others contribute in different ways to the research and service components of the mission. The University of Delaware has developed a particularly useful way of displaying this information in Budget Support Notebooks that we more fully describe in chapter 9.

Other Financial Assessments

In assessing the overall financial effectiveness of a college or university, the National Association of College and University Business Officers offers a particularly useful tool. Frederick J. Turk and Frederick J. Praeger authored

multiple editions of *Ratio Analysis in Higher Education: Measuring Past Performance to Chart Future Direction,* the most recent version of which was published in 1999. That volume was replaced in 2005 by one developed by three financial consulting firms: KPMG; Prager, Sealy & Co.;and BearingPoint, and titled *Strategic Financial Analysis for Higher Education (Sixth Edition)*

Ratio analysis uses information from an institution's audited financial statements to address specific questions that relate to a college's or university's financial health. The earlier versions of *Ratio Analysis in Higher Education* dealt separately with schools under the Governmental Accounting Standards Board (typically public, state-assisted institutions) and those under the Financial Accounting Standards Board (typically privately chartered institutions and a few state-related institutions, such as the University of Delaware). The newer publication, *Strategic Financial Analysis for Higher Education (Sixth Edition)*, deals with both types of institutions.. The specific questions addressed through the ratio analysis approach include the following:

1. Are the financial resources of the institution sufficient to support its mission?

- Is the institution clearly financially healthy or not as of the balance sheet date?

- Is the reporting institution financially

better off or not at the end of the year than it was at the beginning?

- Did the institution live within its financial means during the year?

2. What financial resources are available to support the institution's mission?

- Which resources are internally generated to support the mission?

- Which resources are externally generated to support the mission?

- How does the use of debt support the mission?

3. How are financial resources used to support the institution's mission?

- How are resources used to conduct core educational services?

- How are resources used to conduct educational support services?

- How are resources used to conduct general support services?

4. Are financial resources applied efficiently and effectively to support the institution's mission?

These questions are obviously central to the effective management of a college or university and should be of interest not only to senior administrators at the institution. Responses to the questions are also a means of clearly communicating financial assessments to trustees, external accreditors, bond rating agencies, and other audiences. The inherent beauty of ratio analysis is that it is totally credible—it utilizes audited data from the institution's financial statements.

Let's look at a specific example of ratio analysis. In responding to the question as to whether financial resources are sufficient to support the institutional mission, the first assessment would be what is termed a "viability ratio," which examines whether an institution's available net assets can cover its existing debt. The ratio is expressed as:

$$\frac{\text{Expendable Net Assets}}{\text{Long-Term Debt}}$$

The numerator includes the following components: unrestricted net assets (URNA); temporarily restricted net assets (TRNA); property, plant, and equipment (P/P/E); and plant debt (including all notes, bonds, and leases payable to finance those fixed assets). Expressed as a formula, Expendable Net Assets = URNA + TRNA – (P/P/E – Plant Debt). The denominator, Long-Term Debt, includes the following components: notes payable, bonds payable, and leases payable.

Each of the components of the viability ratio was readily apparent on the University of Delaware's audited fiscal year 2004 Statement of Financial Position and produced the following:

$$\frac{\$809,456,000}{\$169,091,000}$$

The ratio of 4.78 represents the university's potential capacity to use its available expendable assets to eliminate its long-term debt nearly five times over, clearly a strong financial position. This ratio would be of great interest, for example, to any agency that might wish to finance a major capital project at the institution.

This example illustrates the simplicity and credibility of ratio analysis as well as its ability to powerfully communicate assessment of financial position to noneconomists and nonaccountants. It is a form of financial assessment that should be in the repertoire of all institutions and one that easily lends itself to benchmarking for strategic planning purposes.

Assessing Facilities/Physical Resource Progress

While it might seem unnecessary to maintain an assessment program for buildings and other capital assets, it is important to remember that, in the final analysis, state-of-the-art teaching, research, and service depend upon state-of-the-art classrooms, laboratories, and outreach facilities. While our discussion of ratio analysis dealt with financial assessments largely related to core mission operations at an institution, the ratio analysis/strategic financial analysis books available through NACUBO have

suggested a number of ratios that are useful in assessing the maintenance of the physical plant. The first of these is exactly that—a Maintenance Ratio that comprises the following components:

$$\frac{\text{Operation and Maintenance of Plant}}{\text{Education and General Income}}$$

This ratio examines the proportion of revenue that is annually spent on maintaining capital facilities. As with all ratios used in ratio analysis, the Maintenance Ratio should be examined over time to determine trend lines. A steady decline in the magnitude of the ratio signals a decline in institutional commitment to plant upkeep. The consequences of such a trend may be deterioration in the physical plant that might erode faculty and student retention and might have negative consequences for admissions recruiting activity.

Deferred maintenance has historically been a problem on many campuses, particularly with the decline in state support at public institutions and the decline in return on investments at private institutions. Ratio and strategic financial analysis sources previously cited suggest the use of a Deferred Maintenance Ratio to monitor the extent to which this may or may not be a growing problem. The ratio consists of the following components:

$$\frac{\text{Deferred Maintenance}}{\text{Expendable Net Assets}}$$

This ratio focuses on the sum total of a college's or university's outstanding maintenance requirements as a percentage of the institution's expendable net assets. Put quite simply, if this ratio increases over time, it suggests that an institution is choosing to spend expendable resources on functions other than maintenance of the physical plant, and as that plant continues to age, it becomes a genuine liability. We mentioned in chapter 5 the wisdom in annually setting aside 2 percent of the replacement value of the physical plant to address deferred maintenance. To the extent that such set-aside funding is less than 2 percent and approaches zero, the importance of monitoring the Deferred Maintenance Ratio is magnified.

Finally, an thither useful ratio is the Age of Plant Ratio in conjunction with the Deferred Maintenance Ratio. The Age of Plant Ratio includes the following components:

$$\frac{\text{Accumulated Depreciation}}{\text{Depreciation Expense}}$$

This ratio indicates a proxy for the number of years of depreciation that have been applied against the physical plant (accumulated depreciation) as a function of a college's or university's estimation of the life of its facilities. The higher the ratio, the older the plant, requiring ongoing maintenance needs and, where it exists in a major way, serious attention to deferred maintenance.

These three ratios are broad general assessments of the facilities at a college or university. As we suggested in chapter 5, it is also useful to benchmark existing physical space against that at other institutions using the Campus Facilities Inventory, developed and supported by the Society for College and University Planning (SCUP). It is also helpful to examine the campus master plans from peer institutions and aspirational peers to the extent that they are accessible. SCUP has an extensive library of master planning documents available via its Web site at www.scup.org/knowledge/campus_plans.html. The Association for the Advancement of Sustainability in Higher Education (www.aashe.org) has a list of master plans related specifically to the challenges of education for sustainable development and design.

Educational Effectiveness Assessments

Assessing the Student Experience

A broad array of analyses related to students can support both long-term and strategic planning at an institution. Let's look at some examples. In 1986, the University of Delaware initiated a College Student Selection Survey, which was administered to all students to whom an offer of admission was extended. That survey has now been replaced by the commercially prepared Admitted Student Questionnaire, available from the College Board. The survey is administered periodically and collects a broad spectrum of information about the college selection decision, including other schools to which the applicant applied and where the university ranked in the choice hierarchy; perceptions about the university compared with primary competitors; and sources of information and whether it was favorable or unfavorable to the university. The purposes for collecting these data are multiple. First and foremost, the university seeks a better understanding of the reasons that underpin why students choose to attend (what attracted those students to the university?) and, equally important, why students to whom an offer of admission is extended choose to go elsewhere (what are students looking for that the university appears not to offer?). Often, perceptions about an institution shape the college selection decision. The perceptions may be totally inaccurate, but as long as they come into play, they shape the college selection decision. Over the years, the university has gleaned valuable planning information from this survey on dimensions such as the following:

- Students in southern Delaware at one time received less than favorable information about the university from high school guidance counselors. A series of informational breakfasts for guidance counselors in Sussex County corrected the situation.

- Certain groups of academically qualified students received less merit money in the university's financial

aid packages than they received from competitor institutions. This led to the creation of a financial aid model that strategically packages merit aid in a fashion that increases the yield among students with 1250 to 1399 SAT scores, a target population for the university.

- In some instances, a specific land grant admissions competitor was an applicant's first choice, and the University of Delaware ranked second or lower at the time of application. However, in 80 percent of the cases where the applicant visited the University of Delaware campus, they enrolled. This is not an isolated example and led to the restructuring of the Campus Visitation Program.

Institutional research can assist enrollment planners in managing student body size once students have been admitted and enrolled. For example, the Office of Institutional Research and Planning at the University of Delaware has developed two models that assist in monitoring the size of the undergraduate student body. The focus is on undergraduate students, as the size of the graduate population at the institution is consistently between 2,900 and 3,200 students. The Persisters Report, as seen in figure 7.3, is a student tracking model that enables a longitudinal examination of persistence and attrition for first-time freshmen, examining ten entering fall

Figure 7.3: University of Delaware Persisters Report

Enrollment, Dropout Rates, and Graduation Rates for First-Time Freshmen on the Newark Campus: Entering Cohorts 1993 through 2003

Entering Fall Term		Enrollment and Dropout Rates						Graduation Rates			
		1st Fall	2nd Fall	3rd Fall	4th Fall	5th Fall	6th Fall	within 3 yrs	within 4 yrs	within 5 yrs	Total
1991	N	3170	2663	2379	2305	671	116	14	1593	2131	2286
	% enrollment	100.0	84.0	75.0	72.7	21.2	3.7	0.4	50.3	67.2	72.1
	% dropout	0.0	16.0	25.0	26.8	28.6	29.1				
1992	N	2944	2511	2262	2184	561	107	13	1593	2056	2194
	% enrollment	100.0	85.3	76.8	74.2	19.1	3.6	0.4	54.1	69.8	74.5
	% dropout	0.0	14.7	23.2	25.4	26.8	26.5				
1993	N	3181	2688	2392	2306	650	126	15	1621	2139	2295
	% enrollment	100.0	84.5	75.2	72.5	20.4	4.0	0.5	51.0	67.2	72.1
	% dropout	0.0	15.5	24.8	27.0	28.6	28.8				
1994	N	2966	2497	2281	2209	618	97	26	1551	2053	2176
	% enrollment	100.0	84.2	76.9	74.5	20.8	3.3	0.9	52.3	69.2	73.4
	% dropout	0.0	15.8	23.1	24.6	26.9	27.5				
1995	N	3154	2673	2439	2355	599	113	21	1716	2211	2318
	% enrollment	100.0	84.7	77.3	74.7	19.0	3.6	0.7	54.4	70.1	73.5
	% dropout	0.0	15.3	22.7	24.7	26.6	26.3				
1996	N	3290	2804	2585	2489	606	108	22	1822	2299	2400
	% enrollment	100.0	85.2	78.6	75.7	18.4	3.3	0.7	55.4	69.9	72.9
	% dropout	0.0	14.8	21.4	23.7	26.2	26.8				
1997	N	3179	2765	2522	2435	580	118	27	1823	2277	2353
	% enrollment	100.0	87.0	79.3	76.6	18.2	3.7	0.8	57.3	71.6	74.0
	% dropout	0.0	13.0	20.7	22.6	24.4	24.7				
1998	N	3545	3080	2830	2762	653	120	22	2075	2605	2605
	% enrollment	100.0	86.9	79.8	77.9	18.4	3.4	0.6	58.5	73.5	73.5
	% dropout	0.0	13.1	20.2	21.5	23.0	23.1				
1999	N	3513	3126	2870	2757	531	0	31	2168	--	2168
	% enrollment	100.0	89.0	81.7	78.5	15.1	0.0	0.9	61.7	61.7	
	% dropout	0.0	11.0	18.3	20.6	23.2	0.0				
2000	N	3128	2738	2524	2459	0	0	24	--	--	24
	% enrollment	100.0	87.5	80.7	78.6	0.0	0.0	0.8	0.8		
	% dropout	0.0	12.5	19.3	20.6	0.0	0.0				
2001	N	3334	2955	2737	0	0	0	--	--	--	0
	% enrollment	100.0	88.6	82.1	0.0	0.0	0.0	0.0			
	% dropout	0.0	11.4	17.9	0.0	0.0	0.0				
2002	N	3400	3059	0	0	0	0	--	--	--	0
	% enrollment	100.0	90.0	0.0	0.0	0.0	0.0	0.0			
	% dropout	0.0	10.0	0.0	0.0	0.0	0.0				

cohorts at a time. The tracking model also provides graduation rates within four years, after four years, after five years, and beyond. The cohorts are analyzed in total and by sex, Delaware resident/nonresident status, and student ethnicity. The data provide valuable information in identifying specific student groupings that, if not at risk with respect to attrition/nongraduation, are less successful than others. This information yields a basis for further institutional research into student progress or lack of progress.

Cohort survival analysis predicated on data from models such as the Persisters Report has long been a staple in institutional research. However, it has been the experience at the many colleges and universities that cohort survival has not been a highly accurate tool in enrollment projection. Underlying reasons for this phenomenon are factors such as the fact that 25 percent, on average, of any entering freshman cohort does not declare a major. Until a major field of study is identified, frequently after two or more semesters depending upon the prerequisites for that major, progression to degree cannot be assessed. Consequently, student graduation within eight semesters is highly unlikely. In addition, with "stopping out" no longer a rare student behavior, enrollment forecasting predicated on cohort survival is highly problematic. The University of Delaware's Office of Institutional Research and Planning has developed

an enrollment projection model that is predicated on total undergraduate student body attrition rates, continuing rates, and returning rates, using a weighted average for a three-year time frame. The model predicts full-time and part-time students, by Delaware resident/nonresident status. Over the past decade, the model has predicted enrollments by term within 1 percent of the actual number. The model has become the basis for a number of important university estimates, including semester and fiscal year tuition revenue and housing occupancy rates.

Simply knowing numbers of potential and actual students is but the start of a serious program of assessment measures related to student success and satisfaction. During summer orientation, first-time freshmen and transfers at many institutions are administered a survey such as the ACT College Student Needs Assessment Survey, which asks students to identify those knowledge content and skills areas where they feel they will need assistance during their academic careers. This survey assists the academic affairs and student affairs units at the institution in ensuring that their services are in line with the perceived and actual needs of students. Institutional research or assessment offices then typically follow up with these students, surveying them at regular intervals to determine the extent to which they feel that their needs are, in fact, being addressed.

ACT fully understands the differentiated

missions between two-year and four-year institutions and has developed a cadre of survey instruments specifically designed for two-year college use, such as the ACT College Student Needs Assessment Survey. Readers from two-year institutions are encouraged to review the list of instruments available from ACT at www.act.org/ess/twoyear.html. Noel-Levitz also has instrumentation developed for different higher education sectors that can be reviewed at www.noellevitz.com/Our+Services.

Surveys of the type just described are best administered on cyclical basis, such as alternate years or every three or four years, as response patterns change only incrementally from year to year. Resources for assessments are frequently limited, and data should be collected on timing cycles that yield usable information, not simply for the sake of having it on file.

There are a number of different surveys for communicating with students currently enrolled at the institution and for gathering information that assists planners in enhancing student experiences. One example is the National Survey of Student Engagement (NSSE), housed at Indiana University in Bloomington, which asks students to describe a broad range of experiences both in and out of the classroom, the ways in which they learn, the skills that they apply to their studies, and the extent to which experiences at the university are contributing to the development of knowledge, skills, and personal development in specific areas. The survey also asks students for a self-assessment of the extent to which they have gained in selected cognitive and social skills as the result of their university experience. While NSSE is usually administered to freshmen and seniors at most institutions to determine differences in student engagement at the two levels, the University of Delaware oversamples the undergraduate population to include sophomores and juniors. This facilitates an assessment of the apparent maturation process with respect to student engagement as students progress from freshman through senior year. It also allows for comparison of those measures with national benchmarks. All of the data yield highly useful information for faculty and academic planners about the various ways students learn through their experiences at the institution. The data are used in curriculum design, in development of academic and student support services, and in enhancing the quality of student life at the university. An important feature of NSSE is the capability to benchmark institutional scores against aggregate scores from comparable institutions based upon institutional classification. It is also possible to participate in voluntary data sharing consortia with other specific institutions participating in NSSE in any given year.

It is important to note that a companion instrument to NSSE is designed specifically to assess learning styles and levels of engagement for students at two-year colleges. The Community College Survey of Student Engagement (CCSSE) takes into account the very different mission of two-year versus four-year institutions and structures assessment wholly appropriate to that group of students. Benchmarking capabilities comparable to NSSE are also available for CCSSE.

Another student-oriented assessment tool is the Survey of Student Opinions, which is a new instrument from ACT. This survey collects data similar to the older ACT Student Opinion Survey in that it seeks feedback on the extent to which students use, and are satisfied with, specific programs and services at an institution (e.g., library, computing services, registrar, financial aid, food service, and parking). This instrument also measures the extent to which students are satisfied with some 43 dimensions of student life (e.g., quality of academic advising, quality of instruction in the major field, availability of courses, classroom and student activity facilities, and administrative services to students). The new Survey of Student Opinions asks for those measures but also asks students to estimate a series of cognitive and social gains resulting from their academic experience and affords an opportunity for validating some of the impressions

gleaned from the NSSE. As is the case with NSSE, an added value is the capability to benchmark against mean scores from aggregations of comparable institutions, thereby providing additional context for examining and understanding an institution's own discrete scores.

It is worth noting, however, that the greatest value to the university from the Survey of Student Opinions and/or the Student Opinion Survey comes from subsequent creative analyses usually done by an office of institutional research. For example, at the University of Delaware, during the fall term following survey administration, the respondent pool is segmented into two groups: those students who took the survey in the spring and returned in the fall and those students who took the survey in the spring, did not graduate, and did not return in the fall. The university has had less than satisfactory experiences with after-the-fact surveys administered to withdrawing, nonreturning students, and it has found that segmenting the respondent pool for student opinion surveys in the aforementioned fashion yields far more useful information about significantly different response patterns between returning and nonreturning students.

Students who plan to leave the university for any reason generally know they will do so in the spring, and the data collected generally underscores the reasons underlying that decision.

The information helps faculty and administrators understand and address the nonacademic reasons for student attrition. For example, academic advising has been an issue over the years for both returning and nonreturning students at the University of Delaware. As a result, the Office of Institutional Research and Planning is developing a program for administering the ACT Survey of Academic Advising to understand the underlying causes of student dissatisfaction more fully. The results will provide assistance in crafting appropriate administrative response to enhance the advising function.

Yet another area where institutional research can assist planners is postgraduation data collection. Many institutions administer surveys to students upon graduation and at appropriate intervals thereafter. The purpose of these surveys is to gather as much information as possible on the postcommencement activity of each graduating class, e.g., full- or part-time employment in a curriculum-related or non-curriculum-related position; graduate school (often requesting the specific school attended); military service; some other form of voluntary service (Americorps or Job Corps); or involuntarily unemployed. Many institutions supplement these student surveys with employer surveys that utilize information from the career planning office on campus to identify recruiters and to follow up with

information requests as to satisfaction with student preparation and skills. Institutional research offices also provide feedback to campus planners by surveying alumni at regular intervals to gather information on career paths and the extent to which their college or university experience remains relevant to their working life and to their understanding of and contributions to the larger society.

While these examples illustrate the value of surveys and student-oriented assessments, they are not exhaustive. We encourage readers to obtain a copy of the publication *Measuring Quality: Choosing Among Surveys and Other Assessments of College Quality* by Victor Borden and Jody Zak, (published in 2001 by the American Council on Education and the Association for Institutional Research). A joint publication of the American Council on Education and the Association for Institutional Research, the volume describes 30 different national surveys and assessment instruments. Interested parties can contact either sponsoring organization, and a PDF version is available at airweb. org/ under the Publications button.

Finally, while much of this discussion of benchmarking has focused on four-year college examples, there is an innovative benchmarking project specifically designed for two-year institutions. The National Community College Benchmark Project, housed at Johnson

County Community College in Overland Park, Kansas, has created a data collection instrument for benchmarking a broad array of variables reflecting two-year college operations. These include the following:

- Certificate, degree completion, and transfer rates

- Credit course persistence rates

- Performance in transfer institutions

- Student satisfaction and engagement ratings

- Student goal attainment

- College-level course retention and success rates

- Developmental course retention and success rates

- Developmental student success in first college-level courses

- Career program completers' employment status and employer ratings

- Success rates in core academic skill areas

- Institution-wide grade information

- Minority participation rates

- High school graduate enrollment rates

- Market penetration rates

- Business and industry productivity

- Average credit section size

- Student/faculty ratio

- Distance learning outcomes

- Instructional faculty load

- Cost per credit hour and FTE student

- Distance learning sections and grade distributions

- Student/student services staff ratio

- Human resources statistics

- Cost per credit hour

- Training expenditures per employee

Interested readers can learn more about the project at www.nccbp.org.

A final comment: Many of the examples of institutional research described in this volume reflect research being done at the University of Delaware. While Delaware has an institutional research staff of six professionals, the size of the office reflects the size and complexity of the institution. All of the analyses described thus far can be done by smaller institutional research staffs. The key is to communicate with senior leadership on campus to determine which projects are of the greatest strategic value to decision makers. While an institutional research office (including the University of Delaware's) may not be able to do all of the analyses described in this volume, that is not an excuse for doing nothing. The key is communication and consensus on the types of information that are important.

Academic Program Review

It is common practice, often mandated by governing bodies, for institutions to review academic programs regularly and systematically within the institutional curriculum. The reviews typically occur at regular intervals—every five to ten years—and constitute a "mini-self-study" at the academic department level. The academic program under analysis is carefully studied and analyzed to assess its continuing viability and quality. Instruction, scholarship, and service might reflect the broad categories of inquiry in an academic program review. Within each category, a variety of questions might be asked and various measures of success and quality are reviewed.

Under the category of instruction, an academic program review might focus on some or all of the following questions: Is there measurable demand for courses within the program? Is demand increasing, decreasing, or steady? Does the demand come from program majors or from nonmajors? Are teaching loads appropriately administered? Benchmarking projects such as the Delaware Study of Instructional Costs and Productivity help academic departments/programs assess their teaching loads compared with true peers and aspirational peers. Where significant disparities are found between institutional workloads and peer benchmarks, are they are intentional, e.g., the result of deliberate policies restricting class size? Is there demonstrable evidence of student learning?

Our subsequent discussions of

assessment of student learning outcomes indicate that measuring student learning goes well beyond simple grade distributions in departmental courses. Faculty frequently choose from menus involving such strategies as pre- and post-testing, electronic portfolios, undergraduate research projects, senior theses, and capstone courses. High-quality academic programs have carefully reasoned and well-planned strategies for implementing multiple measures of student learning. And, equally important, the results from these multiple measures are *used* as feedback for further academic planning, including curriculum redesign or enhancement and refinement of teaching workloads well as administrative decisions with respect to resource allocation and, as appropriate, facilities design and/or renovation.

Under the categories of scholarship and service, an academic program review might focus on some or all of the following: How are faculty spending their time outside the classroom? What are the department's/program's explicit expectations with respect to faculty scholarship and service? Are faculty accessible to students, either electronically or in person, outside the classroom? Are faculty engaged in either designing new curricula or teaching pedagogies, or refining existing courses? Are faculty in this unit productive with respect to publishing and other forms of scholarly activity? How frequently is their work cited by other scholars? If the unit has potential access to external funds, is the level of contract and grant activity appropriate? How productive are the unit's faculty when compared with true peers and aspirational peers?

The same questions can be posed with respect to activities in the areas of institutional and public service. As is the case with instruction, benchmarking can be helpful in assessing scholarship and service activity. Again, it is of primary importance that the results of all of these assessments be *used* to shape program policy with respect to how faculty are engaged when not in the classroom.

Student Learning Outcomes Assessment

It is important to know the proportion of an entering cohort of first-time freshmen who are retained at a college or university and who ultimately graduate from that institution and, of those graduates, the proportion who find employment or go on to graduate school. However, these measures have little meaning unless accompanied by an assessment of the intellectual tools that students take with them as they move on to postgraduation life. Did the college or university experience change the student with respect to intellectual, social, and cultural measures? Can we empirically demonstrate that students have actually learned in meaningful ways in the academic disciplines in which they elected to study?

As we noted earlier, each of the six

major regional accrediting associations in the United States explicitly calls for assessment of student learning outcomes. Planning for such assessments is not trivial; it requires a clear understanding of what is expected in the way of measures and clear strategies for attaining those measures. The Middle States Commission on Higher Education has articulated the fundamental elements of assessment of student learning to assist colleges and universities in their region. These fundamental elements include the following:

- clearly articulated statements of expected student learning outcomes . . . at all levels (institution, degree/program, course) and for all programs that aim to foster student learning and development...

- a documented, organized, and sustained assessment process to evaluate and improve student learning...

- assessment results that provide sufficient, convincing evidence that students are achieving key institutional and program learning outcomes;

- evidence that student learning assessment information is shared and discussed with appropriate constituents and is used to improve teaching and learning; and

- documented use of student learning assessment information as part of institutional assessment.[48]

48. Middle States Commission on Higher Education, *Characteristics of Excellence in Higher Education: Eligibility Requirements and Standards for Accreditation* (Philadelphia: Middle States Commission on Higher Education, 2006), 66–67.

Planning for an assessment program that contains each of these five elements must be done within the context of an institution's own culture. First and foremost, assessment of student learning outcomes must be owned by the faculty. It is not something that can be done well only because the regional or professional accrediting agency, the president, or the provost said to do it. It must be a process that is developed by faculty for faculty with the explicit purpose of improving instruction and enhancing student learning. In the first decade of the 21st century, this noble objective is not a universal reality, and that is where the planning comes in. The following issues need to be addressed:

- How does an institution bring reluctant faculty into the assessment process?

- How does the institution define and articulate clear, well-understood, and *measurable* learning objectives at the institutional, college, department, and course level, ensuring that each is consistent with mission?

- How does the institution intend to measure those objectives, and how will those measurements be reported at each organizational level to ensure that they are used to improve institutional effectiveness, instruction, and student learning?

This volume is not a handbook on assessing student outcomes; there are extensive and excellent existing resources for that purpose. However, there are a number of planning issues related to student learning outcomes assessment that we should mention here. Staffing for student outcomes assessment is the first planning issue. Is there resident expertise on campus, or is an external search necessary? The assessment office or the assessment component of another existing office requires an individual who can effectively work with individual faculty, departments/programs as total entities, colleges, and, where appropriate, the university as a whole in articulating learning objectives that are consistent with mission. Moreover, that individual needs to work with those parties in determining how the achievement of learning goals should best be assessed. Are course-embedded assessments appropriate? Electronic portfolios? Capstone courses? Undergraduate research projects? Senior theses? Combinations of these? Certainly the assessment tools and strategies for a philosophy department are different from those for chemical engineering or business administration. In addition to the requisite expertise for helping faculty to make these determinations, the individual responsible for student learning outcomes assessment should be an evangelist, attempting to convert reluctant faculty through persuasion and demonstration that measuring student learning is a tool for improving teaching and for understanding and sharing knowledge about teaching effectiveness.

This persuasion can occur only if it is manifestly apparent that assessment data are being used at all levels in the institution to make that college or university more effective, particularly with respect to teaching and learning. To achieve this, assessment data, once collected, must be appropriately analyzed and clearly presented. Once again, a strong institutional research capability is crucial. This presents something of a dilemma for those planning an assessment strategy for a college or university. We made the point earlier that student learning outcomes assessment falls clearly within the realm of faculty responsibilities and needs to be "owned" by the faculty. But colleges and universities are also responsible for developing strategies for assessing institutional effectiveness, which includes a broad range of administrative, fiscal, and facilities analyses. Some larger, more complex institutions such as the University of Delaware have created two separate entities to address assessment activity. The Office of Institutional Research and Planning, reporting to the executive vice president and treasurer, focuses its analytical activity largely on assessing institutional effectiveness. Learning outcomes assessment is housed in the Office of Undergraduate Studies, which reports to the provost. The determination was made that learning outcomes assessment needed to be housed within academic affairs, specifically within an office that concentrates on faculty development. Because the Office of Undergraduate Studies, which also houses the Center

for Teaching Effectiveness, enjoys respect and credibility among the faculty, the move toward assessment is facilitated. The Office of Institutional Research and Planning and the Office of Undergraduate Studies work collaboratively as appropriate (e.g., survey design and drawing samples), but the role of each office in the overall assessment strategy at the institution is quite clear.

Smaller institutions with staff constraints may not have the option of separate entities for assessing institutional effectiveness and student learning outcomes. Typically, these institutional have units with titles such as Office of Institutional Research *and* Assessment. Such an organizational configuration is workable, but it also forces institutional planners to prioritize their analytical needs. Since this type of institutional research entity has to provide analyses in support of assessing institutional effectiveness and student learning outcomes, careful thought and planning must go into defining and articulating what the institution needs from this office and what it is willing to do without. Again, the driving context in making these determinations is the institutional mission.

A Final Word About Assessment

This chapter has described a wide range of strategies and tools for assessing institutional and educational effectiveness. Two important contexts should be at the forefront of assessment activity. While it is important to measure, to the greatest extent possible, all aspects of an institution's operation, it is just as important to have a comparative context for viewing those measures. For example, it is all well and good to have measures of teaching loads and instructional costs at the institution, retention and graduation rates, and measures of student engagement and learning. But how do we know how those measures compare with actual peer institutions and institutions we aspire to be like? Benchmarking is a critical component of comprehensive assessment activity.

Many data collection projects such as the Delaware Study of Instructional Costs and Productivity, the National Survey of Student Engagement, and the Consortium for Student Retention Data Exchange provide not only national benchmark data, but also the capability for participating institutions to specify and define relevant peer groups. This is a capability that colleges and universities should pursue in connection with data collection activity.

There are also natural affinity groups for colleges and universities. The Association of American Universities Data Exchange, the Southern Universities Group, and the Higher Education Data Sharing Consortium (more than 100 private colleges and universities), to name three, provide the opportunity for comparable institutions to share data across a broad range of issues, including learning outcomes assessment. In a similar vein, professional associations may provide a focal point around which institutions can gather and share information. The six regional accrediting bodies, as well as the Association for Institutional Research, are currently focusing on professional development opportunities in the area of learning outcomes assessment. Similarly, the Society for College and University Planning is providing vehicles for assessing physical space issues. Institutions engaging in any type of assessment should seek out as many benchmarking opportunities as possible to determine their relative position within the higher education marketplace.

Chapter 8:

Integrating Planning and Assessment

Planning occurs at multiple levels at a college or university. Academic departments develop plans for curriculum, research, and service, and for deploying both human and fiscal resources directed at achieving planning goals. Administrative units develop plans to support academic and student life, and the economical and efficient operation of the institution as a business enterprise. As we noted in chapter 2, planning at all levels and for all purposes should occur under the overarching umbrella of the institutional mission. However, planning is not a process in which a formula is followed and intended outcomes are realized. It is a dynamic process in which planning goals are carefully crafted within the context of that institutional mission and appropriate, *measurable* planning objectives are articulated to assess progress toward the realization of those goals.

In chapter 6, we looked at specific University of Delaware planning objectives related to the following goal: "The University will continue to attract and retain the most academically talented and diverse undergraduate students, and support their intellectual, cultural, and ethical development as citizens, scholars, and professionals." Let's briefly consider three of those objectives:

1. Maintain a freshman-to-sophomore retention rate above the national average for highly selective institutions, and seek to achieve a consistent rate of 90 percent or higher.

2. Maintain a graduation rate above the national average for highly selective institutions, and seek to achieve a six-year rate of 75 percent or higher.

3. Increase minority and international enrollment, with retention and graduation rates for those populations consistent with university-wide averages for all students.

We saw in chapter 7 that the University of Delaware has a specific assessment tool, the Persisters Report, that enables the institution to track entering cohorts of first-time freshmen for successive fall terms, calculating persistence and graduation rates for each term. The university does not collect these data solely to complete the Integrated Postsecondary Educational Data System (IPEDS) Graduation Rate Survey or the NCAA student-athlete Graduation Success Rate Survey, although the capability to fulfill these reporting obligations is a by-product of this assessment activity. The university collects these data to determine at any given time precisely where it stands in relation to the benchmarks established in the respective planning objectives and,

---

where it falls short of those benchmarks, to determine appropriate strategies to move the institution forward. The data can be disaggregated to calculate retention and graduation rates for Delaware residents compared with nonresidents, for men compared with women, and for all federally recognized ethnic categories. Each of these demographic descriptors is important in contributing to the university's overall retention and graduation rates. The disaggregation into ethnic categories is particularly important to planning objective 3 above, which calls for retention and graduation rates for ethnic minorities that are comparable to the overall student rates. During the late 1980s and 1990s, the university invested substantial resources in academic support programs designed to enhance student success among ethnic minorities. Accurate persistence/graduation data were essential to determining the success of those support programs. In short, assessment data were used to reinforce planning decisions.

The Delaware Study of Instructional Costs and Productivity, referenced in chapter 7, is used not only for faculty and resource allocation decisions at the institutions that participate in the consortium; it is a resource for budgetary decisions at the university system level in states such as North Carolina and Tennessee, among many. Assessment data again underpin planning decisions related to resource allocation, a requirement consistent with accreditation standards across the United States.

Use of assessment data as empirical underpinning for planning decisions is equally important in the area of learning outcomes. For example, suppose an institution wished to initiate or revise a program of general education. Planning begins with an articulation of what an institution specifically means by "general education." At the University of Delaware, general education is viewed as a total, coherent experience embracing specific learning goals around which the institution's academic resources may be organized to optimize the learning environment. The first step is to think through the intended learning goals or outcomes of such a general education program. At this institution, they read as follows:

1. Attain effective skills in oral and written communication, quantitative reasoning, and the use of information technology.

2. Learn to think critically to solve problems.

3. Be able to work and learn both independently and collaboratively.

4. Engage questions of ethics and recognize responsibilities to self, community, and society at large.

5. Understand the diverse ways of thinking that underlie the search for knowledge in the arts, humanities, sciences, and social sciences.

6. Develop the intellectual curiosity, confidence, and engagement that will

lead to lifelong learning.

7. Develop the ability to integrate academic knowledge with experiences that extend the boundaries of the classroom.

8. Expand understanding and appreciation of human creativity and diverse forms of aesthetic and intellectual expression.

9. Understand the foundations of United States society including the significance of its cultural diversity.

10. Develop an international perspective in order to live and work effectively in an increasingly global society.[49]

The articulation of these learning goals should be a product primarily of discussions among faculty, but should include academic support and student life personnel as well as appropriate administrative personnel. Good planning seeks the broadest possible input leading to a range of implementation solutions. In other words, having identified these ten learning goals, how does the institution effectively realize them?

A common tool for delivering general education courses has come to be known as the freshman-year experience. Precisely what constitutes that experience and how it is delivered is a function of academic planning. The planning community at the University of Delaware embraced not only faculty, but personnel from the Office

of Undergraduate Studies, Office of Residence Life, Study Abroad Programs, and other key support offices across campus. Depending upon the academic major selected by an incoming freshman, a number of first-year experiences are available:

• First Year Seminars. These are discipline-specific courses that introduce freshmen to the expectations within the academic major and career possibilities upon graduation. This is not an introductory survey course; it is a guide to academic survival within the discipline, ensuring that students know at the outset precisely what will be required of them during their undergraduate careers.

• Learning Integrated Freshman Experience (LIFE). LIFE freshmen form a small learning community organized around several of their academic courses in which the students are coenrolled. There is also a central academic theme as well as out-of-class experiences related to coursework and the academic theme. The LIFE courses and experiences are referred to as LIFE clusters, which involve an integration of a variety of experiences centered on academic material. Some clusters focus on specific majors, others on a more general focus. Most clusters require that the students

---

49. University of Delware, "Ten Goals of Undergraduate Education," Newark, DE, www.ugs.udel.edu/gened/Ten_Goals/Goals.htm.

live together. First-year students are assigned to a cluster and to the same residence hall community. The students are coenrolled in the cluster courses as well as a cocurricular course, University 101. Each cluster has a peer mentor, an advanced undergraduate student who helps students make the adjustment to university academic life and ensures seriousness of purpose and academic quality in the cocurricular experiences of LIFE students. Each cluster also has a LIFE mentor, who provides counsel for the cluster and helps the peer mentor and students in the cluster explore academic issues related to the cluster theme.

- Pathways courses. Pathways courses at the University of Delaware, which are part of the Delaware General Education Initiative, are one model of general education at the university designed to provide integrated academic learning experiences for new students. Pathways courses are thematic, integrative courses for first-year students designed to introduce the academic resources of the university and to teach basic intellectual skills required for a successful undergraduate experience. Often designed collaboratively by teams of faculty from different disciplines, Pathways courses offer students some exciting opportunities to approach topics of general interest from cross-, inter-, or multidisciplinary perspectives.

- Discovery Learning Experience. As a part of the signature experience at the university, all students participate in a Discovery Learning Experience, experiential learning that involves instructional experiences out of class and beyond typical curriculum courses. These enrichment experiences exist for students under the supervision of a faculty member. Discovery Learning Experience includes internship, service learning, independent study, undergraduate research, and study abroad. The Discovery Learning Experience also frequently serves as a capstone to the general education program.

While each of these options, along with the Honors Program Colloquia, may differ in method, all are intended to enable first-year students to:

- Participate in a community of students with common interests and goals.

- Become familiar with the University of Delaware and its various student resources.

- Learn about opportunities after graduation in their field of interest through activities such as field trips, conversations with practitioners, and on- and off-campus experiences, such as internships and service-learning projects.

- Participate in a group-based project with a public presentation that applies what has been learned in a course common to members of the community of students.

- Practice and improve academic, oral, and written communication skills necessary for a successful and rewarding college experience.

- Develop a better understanding of academic ethics.

- Reflect in discussion and written form on changes to the student learning process and academic expectations.

- Get to know faculty.

Having carefully planned the delivery system for implementing general education, the university's next critical step is evaluating the extent to which the delivery system is enabling students to achieve the ten stated learning outcomes. It is important to underscore that, when developing an assessment strategy to measure learning outcomes, institutional effectiveness, or any other dimension of the operation of a college or university, there is no one-size-fits-all approach. While it might prove tempting to take a cookbook approach to assessment—simply follow the recipe and enjoy the product—this fails to account for the differences in institutional missions, faculty training, student preparedness, institutional cultures, and a host of other dimensions across postsecondary institutions. Just as years of planning went into the identification of appropriate general education learning outcomes and delivery systems at the University of Delaware, equal time and energy must

go into the development of assessment strategies that reflect those outcomes and delivery systems.

This is not rocket science; we are not suggesting that every college and university in the United States needs to reinvent the wheel as it develops an approach to outcomes assessment. What we are suggesting, however, is that the tools and measurement strategies selected must be appropriate to the institution's culture. For example, the University of Delaware opted to use LIFE clusters as one vehicle for delivering general education. Given the nature of the LIFE program, it is not sufficient simply to measure student learning in the classroom. A residence life dimension needs to be addressed, as does the peer mentoring component. Cognitive gains in those courses must include an assessment of whether students write better as the result of the courses. In short, assessment strategies must measure the full range of what is occurring within an academic program.

In assessing a general education program such as that of the University of Delaware, there are a number of approaches to measurement:

1. Student performance in courses. More than simple grade distribution in specific required general education courses, it is important to assess through multiple measures the extent to which students have grown intellectually and are able to demonstrate clear cognitive gains.

This evidence may be garnered through capstone experiences, internships/cooperative education experiences, and field work in experiential courses.

2. Cognitive student surveys. Colleges and universities commonly use pre- and posttesting instruments, from vendors such as ACT and the Educational Testing Service, that are specifically designed to measure gains in general education skills areas. Other tools, such as the Watson-Glaser Critical Thinking Appraisal, provide additional information on student gains.

3. Student surveys. There is a host of survey instruments designed to measure student needs and satisfaction, and to enable self-estimates of gains in cognitive and social skills. The National Survey of Student Engagement asks students to describe their academic and intellectual experiences, learning/mental activities, social interactions, and other characteristics, and affords students the opportunity to estimate gains in specific skills areas. The ACT Survey of Student Opinions provides similar opportunities for students to self-report skills gains, and also focuses on satisfaction with academic and student support services. This is particularly appropriate for a general education strategy such as the LIFE clusters, which involve residence halls and other areas of student life. Pre- and posttesting with an instrument such as the ACT College Student Needs Assessment Survey gathers information on areas where entering students feel they need assistance (e.g., quantitative reasoning, critical thinking, oral and written communication, and library and computer skills), with follow-up to determine the extent to which the institution has addressed those needs. These surveys can be used to enrich the baseline information gathered from measures of student course performance and cognitive measures.

4. Institutional research. Tried and true institutional research practices such as cohort survival are valuable. Do students whose first-year experience includes LIFE clusters persist at different rates from those who do not? The same can be asked for students who enroll in Pathways courses or the First Year Seminars. It is also useful to follow these students beyond the freshman year to determine if the groundwork provided by specific general education experiences results in different persistence and graduation patterns.

While assessment is a critical component of the academic planning process, its value is realized only when the assessment data are *used* to improve programmatic offerings and student performance. Assessment is simply a feedback loop in the planning process, enabling planners to identify what works and what does not, and to make appropriate adjustments—including resource allocation decisions—directed at more fully realizing the stated planning objectives. This approach to implementing and assessing general education is but one example. New teaching pedagogies lend themselves to planning for implementation and assessment of effectiveness. Is problem-based learning more effective in certain disciplines than others? Is service learning appropriate for all academic majors? These questions are the framework around which academic planning and assessment are structured, and in answering them it is important to acquire multiple measures, i.e., more than a single assessment strategy, to ensure cross-validation of results.

Just as the linkage between planning and assessment is intended to improve program offerings and student performance, administrative planning lends itself to assessment with an eye toward improving institutional efficiency. There is no point in engaging in survey research using the College Board's Admitted Student Questionnaire unless the responses gleaned from nonenrolling students who were admitted to the institution are used to better understand perceptions of the institution within the admissions marketplace and how students make the college selection decision. Chapter 7 provided a broad range of assessment strategies in support of institutional and academic planning. However, for assessment to be useful,

the data generated from analytical activity must be used to enhance and improve the planning process. Chapter 9 describes a case study example of planning and assessment that has been effectively linked to enhance institutional effectiveness at a major research university that had experienced rough seas over a protracted period of time.

Getting Started and Getting Help

While this discussion of examples integrating assessment into the planning process is fairly straightforward, institutions with little or no experience in strategic planning may still find the process daunting. In those instances, it is possible to secure assistance.

Many institutions, when setting out to implement a strategic planning/outcomes assessment process, elect to use the services of a consultant. In choosing a consultant, it is important to articulate specifically the institution's needs to ensure a fit between those needs and the consultant's skills. Where does one find consultants? A useful starting point is to ask colleagues at other institutions for recommendations, and once names have been received, to ask the consultants for references. Consulting fees typically run into the thousands per day plus expenses, so it makes no sense to hire an individual without a clear understanding of that consultant's record.

Organizations such as the Society for College and University Planning and the Association for Institutional Research typically have consultants among their membership. However, neither organization recommends individuals, as doing so constitutes a tacit endorsement of that individual. Perusing the organizational directory will yield consultant's names, and it is up to the contracting institution to do the legwork in obtaining references.

Another strategy is to contact colleagues within the accrediting community to ask for the names of other comparable institutions that have implemented exemplary planning and assessment processes. Our experience over the years has been that higher education institutions are quite collegial when it comes to sharing processes that work. The operative word in selecting exemplary institutions is *comparable*. Because of obvious organizational and structural differences in complexity between a baccalaureate institution of 900 students and a research university with 35,000 students, it would be folly to expect the same planning/assessment strategies at both institutions. That said, a humanities department at the research university may find electronic portfolio assessment in place at the baccalaureate institution to be a useful evaluation strategy. The key is to make clear precisely what your institutional needs are.

In summary, there are a number of ways to secure assistance in structuring the planning/assessment process at a college or university. However, the process involves more than a simple telephone call. It requires time and energy to ensure a real fit between the institution's needs and the services being offered. Where that time and energy is wisely spent, a successful outcome is much more likely.

Chapter 9

Planning and Assessment at the University of Delaware: A Case Study

How do the discussions of academic, resource, and facilities planning articulated thus far come together in the actual life of a college or university? An extended case study example illustrates the importance of looking carefully at how goals are identified, initiatives are selected, resource allocation decisions are made, and results are reported back to the community.

The University of Delaware is a research/doctoral-extensive institution, annually enrolling more than 16,000 undergraduate students and 3,300 graduate students. However, this was not always the university's enrollment profile. As recently as 1965, the university enrolled 5,160 undergraduates; that number grew to 14,370 in 1988 (the choice of 1988 is pointed, as we will discuss shortly). The university's growth in enrollment during that twenty-three-year period was not an exercise in enrollment planning. During the 1970s and early 1980s, the institution enjoyed enormous demand for undergraduate seats, while at the same time growing the number of graduate programs and recruiting research faculty to teach in those graduate programs. Recurring expenditures such as faculty and administrative salaries during this period of explosive growth were frequently

covered by simply ratcheting up the number of undergraduates admitted in a given year. While tuition dollars are a recurring revenue source, those dollars that fall outside a carefully constructed enrollment/tuition revenue projection model are not. When the bottom fell out of the baby boom college enrollment bubble in the 1980s, the university found itself in difficult financial straits.

In 1987, the University of Delaware embarked on a comprehensive long-range planning process referred to as Project Vision. Over a period of 18 months, the campus developed a planning document with a broad range of planning goals and measurable objectives running the full gamut of functional areas. The campus community reviewed and revised the institutional mission statement and achieved a measure of consensus on planning goals and objectives. Just as the planning document neared completion, two unforeseen events took place. The president who shepherded Project Vision suddenly resigned his office, and the Delaware and regional economies settled into a deep recession.

By 1988, the University of Delaware found itself with nearly $9 million in recurring expenditures on nonrecurring revenue sources. A new administration was intent on rectifying this situation

Figure 9.1: Budget Support Data--Philosophy

BUDGET SUPPORT DATA   College of Arts and Sciences
1996-97 Through 1998-99   Humanities Department

A. TEACHING WORKLOAD DATA

	FALL 1996	FALL 1997	FALL 1998	SPRING 1997	SPRING 1998	SPRING 1999
FTE MAJORS						
Undergraduate	38	31	39	38	40	39
Graduate	0	0	0	0	0	0
Total	38	31	39	38	40	39
DEGREES GRANTED						
Bachelor's	-----	-----	-----	20	19	19
Master's	-----	-----	-----	0	0	0
Doctorate	-----	-----	-----	0	0	0
TOTAL	-----	-----	-----	20	19	19
STUDENT CREDIT HOURS						
Lower Division	6,246	5,472	5,448	4,518	6,156	5,478
Upper Division	726	638	869	1,159	951	966
Graduate	183	153	129	195	276	135
Total	7,155	6,263	6,446	5,872	7,383	6,579
% Credit Hours Taught by Faculty on Appointment	77%	81%	77%	82%	91%	82%
% Credit Hours Taught by Supplemental Faculty	23%	19%	23%	18%	9%	18%
% Credit Hours Consumed by Nonmajors	98%	97%	98%	96%	98%	97%
FTE STUDENTS TAUGHT						
Lower Division	416	365	363	301	410	365
Upper Division	48	43	58	77	63	64
Graduate	20	17	14	22	31	15
Total	485	424	435	400	504	445
FTE FACULTY						
Department Chair	1.0	1.0	1.0	1.0	1.0	1.0
Faculty on Appointment	15.0	16.0	15.0	15.0	15.0	15.0
Supplemental Faculty	1.5	1.0	1.3	1.0	0.8	1.5
Total	17.5	18.0	17.3	17.0	16.8	17.5
WORKLOAD RATIOS						
Student Credit Hours/FTE Faculty	408.9	347.9	373.7	345.4	440.8	375.9
FTE Students Taught/FTE Faculty	27.7	23.6	25.2	23.5	30.1	25.4

through creation of a budget planning process that would not only balance the budget, but sustain university planning well after balance was achieved.

Budget/Financial Planning

In balancing the budget, it was estimated that approximately 243 full-time equivalent (FTE) positions would have to be removed from the basic operating budget. Beyond eliminating those positions, additional savings had to be achieved. In approaching the budget-planning/budget-balancing process, certain principles were adopted:

- To the greatest extent possible, the academic core of the university—and particularly the instructional

function—would be insulated from substantial budget reductions.

- Administrative reductions would come first through elimination of vacant positions and through retirements and resignations. Thereafter, filled positions would be eliminated in accordance with university termination policies.

- The university would seek to streamline administrative functions and make them more cost-effective and cost-efficient through the widespread introduction of technology into streamlined business practices.

- Budget reductions at the university

Figure 9.1: Budget Support Data--Philosophy

BUDGET SUPPORT DATA
1996–97 Through 1998–99

College of Arts and Sciences
Humanities Department

B. FISCAL DATA

	FY 1996 ($)	FY 1997 ($)	FY 1998 ($)
RESEARCH AND SERVICE			
Research Expenditures	0	5,151	499
Public Service Expenditures	0	0	0
Total Sponsored Research/Service	0	5,151	499
Sponsored Funds/FTE Faculty on Appointment	0	312	31
COST OF INSTRUCTION			
Direct Instructional Expenditures	1,068,946	1,141,927	1,144,585
Direct Expense/Student Credit Hour	81	84	88
Direct Expense/FTE Student Taught	1,198	1,229	1,301
REVENUE MEASURES			
Earned Income from Instruction	3,960,208	4,366,720	4,311,275
Earned Income/Direct Instructional Expense	3.73	3.82	3.77

---

would be targeted to the greatest extent possible. Across-the-board reductions were shunned, as they can lead to across-the-board mediocrity.

Within three years, the university achieved the objective of a supporting recurring expenses with recurring revenues. Budget reductions were achieved under the auspices of a University Budget Council, made up mostly of academic deans and chairs along with some administrative officers. The council was staffed by the director of budget and the director of institutional research and planning. In the final analysis, of the 243 positions that were eliminated, only four were faculty— all non-tenured—in a drastically undersubscribed academic program that was eliminated.

At the same time administrative and academic support reductions were being made, organizational efficiencies were being broadly achieved. Using computerized administrative systems, the institution went from a paper-intensive environment to a business operation that is virtually paperless. As might be anticipated, a number of positions associated with paper-processing activity were eliminated. In addition, the decision was made to outsource a number of functions that were previously university operated, including the bookstore and dining services, and a number of student-support services were moved to auxiliary service status, i.e., self-supporting and off the basic operating budget. These

included the university counseling center and the student centers.

It should not be assumed that, while noninstructional units were bearing the brunt of budget reductions, academic departments continued in business-as-usual fashion. The intent at the University of Delaware was that *all* units would become budget conscious, striving to maximize productivity and cost-effectiveness. As a guide for making annual academic department resource allocations (which did not increase by an across-the-board percentage) the Office of Institutional Research and Planning, in consultation with the academic departments, created what came to be known as the Budget Support Notebook. The notebook provided a summary of productivity measures for each academic department on campus—majors enrolled, degrees granted, student credit hours taught, and FTE students taught. Two key productivity rations were also included— student credit hours taught per FTE faculty and FTE students taught per FTE faculty. The notebook also contained fiscal data—direct research and service expenditures and direct instructional expenditures for the department for each of three fiscal years. The notebook then married the teaching load and fiscal data to arrive at useful comparative ratios, such as direct expense per student credit hour taught and direct expense per FTE student taught.

Figure 9.1 displays budget support data for a department in the humanities. It

Figure 9.2: Budget Support Data—Graduate Science Unit

BUDGET SUPPORT DATA   Graduate Science Unit
1996–97 Through 1998–99

A. TEACHING WORKLOAD DATA

	FALL 1996	FALL 1997	FALL 1998	SPRING 1997	SPRING 1998	SPRING 1999
FTE MAJORS						
Undergraduate	0	0	0	0	0	0
Graduate	75	74	94	72	73	87
Total	75	74	94	72	73	87
DEGREES GRANTED						
Bachelor's	-----	-----	-----	0	0	0
Master's	-----	-----	-----	15	14	15
Doctorate	-----	-----	-----	9	7	9
TOTAL	-----	-----	-----	24	21	19
STUDENT CREDIT HOURS						
Lower Division	210	156	216	0	0	0
Upper Division	10	43	46	70	12	31
Graduate	848	668	759	740	718	696
Total	1,068	867	1,021	810	730	727
% Credit Hours Taught by Faculty on Appointment	96%	96%	95%	95%	95%	92%
% Credit Hours Taught by Supplemental Faculty	4%	4%	5%	5%	5%	8%
% Credit Hours Consumed by Nonmajors	3%	2%	3%	0%	0%	0%
FTE STUDENTS TAUGHT						
Lower Division	14	10	14	0	0	0
Upper Division	1	3	3	5	1	2
Graduate	94	74	84	82	80	77
Total	109	87	102	87	81	79
FTE FACULTY						
Department Chair	0.0	0.0	0.0	0.0	0.0	0.0
Faculty on Appointment	31.0	30.8	28.8	31.0	29.8	27.8
Supplemental Faculty	0.3	0.3	0.3	0.5	0.3	0.3
Total	31.3	31.1	29.1	31.5	30.1	28.1
WORKLOAD RATIOS						
Student Credit Hours/FTE Faculty	34.1	27.9	35.0	25.7	24.2	25.9
FTE Students Taught/FTE Faculty	3.5	2.8	3.5	2.8	2.7	2.8

quickly becomes evident why this sort of information is essential to budget planners. If the only "productivity" measures examined were those actually requested by deans and chairs—FTE majors and degrees granted—a department that has thirty-five to forty majors and that grants about twenty bachelor's degrees per year would be a ripe candidate for budget reduction, if not outright elimination. But the budget support data probe much deeper than that.

The department averages between 6,000 and 7,000 student credit hours taught per term, the vast majority of which are taught by faculty on appointment, i.e., full-time faculty as opposed to adjunct. Clearly, 6,000 student credit hours are not being consumed by the thirty-five humanities majors registered to the department. Indeed, the budget support data indicate that 96 to 98 percent of those student credit hours are being consumed by nonmajors, in most instances satisfying the humanities component of their general education requirements. *Consequently, any decision to reduce resources allocated to the department has the potential for adversely affecting the capability of university students to satisfy general education course requirements.* It is worthy to note that the two instructional productivity ratios—roughly 375 student credit hours and more than twenty-five FTE students taught per FTE faculty— are among the highest at the university.

Looking at the fiscal data, it is not surprising that there are virtually no externally funded research or service expenditures for this department in the humanities. The cost ratios of roughly $85 per student credit hour taught and $1,200 per FTE student taught are among the lowest at the university. The Budget Support Notebook then introduces a revenue measure that is intended to help inform department chairs and faculty of their relative instructional contribution to the university budget. Earned income from instruction is a measure that was developed by the Office of Institutional Research and Planning in collaboration with the Budget Office. Total tuition revenue at the university during a given fiscal year is divided by the total number of student credit hours taught at the university during the same year to arrive at a measure of tuition revenue per student credit hour taught. That unit measure is then multiplied by the number of student credit hours taught in this humanities department to arrive at earned income from instruction. This is then divided by the direct instructional expenditures to arrive at an income-to-expense ratio that, in the instance of this humanities department, is consistently approaching 4.0. What this says is that the department "earns" roughly four times what it costs to operate the department. Keep in mind, however, that we look only at direct instructional expense. Not included is the cost of admitting students to the university, registering them for courses, heating and lighting classrooms, and other costs. The budget support construct was never intended to be a full cost model. It was intended to be an educational and management tool for academic resource allocations. Consequently, when department chairs with an income-to-expense ratio approximating 1.0 insist that they are covering costs, they are told that the ratio would have to be at least 2.0 to cover indirect costs that are not included in the analysis.

It also is instructive to look at a drastically different type of academic unit. Where the humanities department just examined is exclusively baccalaureate and teaches large numbers

---

Figure 9.3: Total Compensation, 1989–90 Compared with 1999–2000

FULL PROFESSOR

Institution	1989–90		1999–2000
Princeton University	91,800	University of Pennsylvania	151,900
University of Pennsylvania	91,500	Princeton University	134,100
Georgetown University	88,700	Georgetown University	126,100
Carnegie Mellon	85,800	Carnegie Mellon	123,200
University of Virginia	85,100	University of Virginia	122,900
George Mason University	84,400	UNIVERSITY OF DELAWARE	116,200
Johns Hopkins University	83,800	Temple University	114,300
New Jersey Institute of Technology	83,100	George Mason University	113,900
Rutgers, New Brunswick/Piscataway	82,000	College of William and Mary	113,400
Lehigh University	80,800	Lehigh University	111,300
University of Maryland, College Park	80,500	American University	111,100
Virginia Polytechnic Institute and State University	76,700	Johns Hopkins University	110,800
University of Maryland, Baltimore	76,700	The George Washington University	110,800
University of Pittsburgh-Main Campus	76,500	New Jersey Institute of Technology	109,200
The George Washington University	76,500	Rutgers, New Brunswick/Piscataway	109,000
American University	76,300	The Pennsylvania State University	108,600
The Pennsylvania State University	75,300	University of Maryland, College Park	106,800
UNIVERSITY OF DELAWARE	74,700	University of Pittsburgh-Main Campus	105,600
College of William and Mary	74,400	Virginia Polytechnic Institute and State University	103,800
Virginia Commonwealth University	72,600	Drexel University	103,700
Drexel University	71,000	Virginia Commonwealth University	103,300
Old Dominion University	70,400	University of Maryland, Baltimore	96,200
Temple University	68,400	Howard University	93,300
The Catholic University of America	64,800	The Catholic University of America	86,800
Howard University	64,000	Old Dominion University	No Report

Source: "Economic Status of the Profession," *Academe*, March–April issue for each respective year.

---

of undergraduates, the graduate science unit (see Figure 9.2) under examination contains no departments and awards only graduate degrees. Like the humanities department, it has few majors, around forty per term, and few degrees granted, roughly twenty per year. However, where the humanities department was averaging 375 student credit hours and more than twenty-five FTE students taught per FTE faculty, the comparable numbers for the graduate science unit are roughly thirty and three, respectively. Moreover, the cost per credit hour taught in graduate science unit is approximately $1,000, compared with $85 in the humanities department. If these were the only data examined, the temptation to slash the science unit budget would be nearly irresistible. However, where externally funded research and service expenditures per FTE faculty were virtually zero in the humanities department, the ratio averages roughly $250,000 per FTE faculty in the graduate science unit. These data illustrate an important facet of the relationship between and

among academic departments and institutional mission. The science unit is exclusively a graduate unit. While graduate instruction in an academic unit in the sciences can be measured to some extent in terms of student credit hours taught, a significant portion of teaching occurs within the context of the interaction in the research laboratory between graduate research assistants and faculty mentors. Research activities generate approximately $250,000 per

faculty member each year. While the instructional income-to-expense ratio for the science unit is among the lowest at the university, the sponsored funds per FTE faculty ratio is among the highest, underscoring the significant contribution of the science unit to supporting the research and service components of the university mission. *Consequently, any significant reduction in resource allocations to this unit may adversely affect the institution's research and service mission.*

The budget support summaries for each department at the university are accessible by all of the other departments. The data upon which resource allocation decisions are made, and upon which academic budget planning is predicated, are transparent to all units. The two departments cited here provide examples of data that have enabled the institution to understand that it is a *uni*versity—one organization with a common mission, rather than a loose confederation of fifty-four fiefdoms, each with its own agenda. The humanities department illustrates the teaching component of the university mission, while the graduate science unit underscores the research and service components.

Long-Range and Strategic Planning

With the unexpected resignation of the university's president, either of two paths of action might have been taken. The planning process could have been scuttled, given the departure of the president and new fiscal challenges, or the Project Vision planning document could be revisited and prioritized. The latter occurred under the guidance of a committee comprising senior chaired professors. When the new university president arrived on campus in 1990, he was presented with that list of planning priorities distilled from the Project Vision document.

The president and his senior staff then defined four strategic goals from the list of planning priorities. While the other planning goals and objectives were not ignored, the following four goals assumed primacy with respect to full realization and allocation of human and fiscal resources:

- Provide competitive compensation for faculty and staff.

- Enhance student access to the university, particularly through undergraduate financial aid.

- Create a more student-centered campus.

- Upgrade buildings and campus infrastructure through the gradual elimination of deferred maintenance.

Each of the four goals is tied to the university's mission. Competitive compensation relates to the university's commitment to retain and attract the brightest and most capable faculty and staff available. Enhanced student access relates to the university's commitment to provide undergraduate and

graduate education to all academically qualified students in Delaware and, with a selective admissions policy, to students from the region and nation. A student-centered campus relates to the university's commitment to provide appropriate academic support and student services to ensure student success and create a more student-friendly environment. State-of-the-art campus facilities are essential to the core mission areas of teaching, research, and service. Having identified these clearly mission-related strategic goals, the next step was developing measurable objectives for assessing progress toward those goals.

The university administration went on public record with the following planning objectives related to the four goal areas:

- Average total compensation for faculty, by academic rank, would be at or above the median *within five years* for the twenty-four Category I doctoral universities against which the University of Delaware benchmarks itself for salary purposes.

- Total undergraduate financial aid from all sources would increase by 100 percent within five years.

- Student satisfaction with programs and services at the university, as measured using the ACT Student Opinion Survey, would demonstrate significant gains within five years.

- The university would commit itself to a policy of annually allocating the equivalent of at least 2 percent of the replacement value of the physical plant to be used for facilities renovation and rehabilitation. While annually allocating 2 percent of the replacement value of the physical plant would allow for complete replacement of the physical infrastructure over a fifty-year period, the university actually expended more than that in most years to catch up on what had been deferred maintenance.

We should emphasize that these strategic goals and objectives were not developed in a vacuum by the president and his senior staff. They were selected from the prioritized list developed by the Faculty Committee on Project Vision. The selection of these four goals was rooted in the choice of what was central to the university's mission and, equally important, what was "do-able" given existing resource constraints. Communicating this to appropriate parties was the next major step in effective planning. Within the university community, Faculty Senate meetings, meetings of other employee groups, the Office of Public Relations, as well as institutional and the student media were

all effectively used to inform the full range of campus constituencies about the strategic initiatives. It should be noted that there are very different audiences with respect to how planning activity is communicated. Faculty and professional staff require more detail about how resources are being reallocated to support planning initiatives than do more transient groups. In communicating with alumni and other external constituencies, particularly donors, it is more important to convey results than the more technical details that drive those results. The university used its broadly circulated alumni magazine to annually update progress on the initiatives.

Results need to be clear, analytical statements of fact. We have noted the importance of an institutional research capability, if not the more desirable option of having an institutional research office per se, to support planning activity. The following "results" for each of the strategic initiatives convey direct institutional research information regarding progress as well as analysis. Figure 9.3 shows competitive compensation for faculty. The key elements of analysis here are

Figure 9.4: Growth in Undergraduate Scholarship Funds at the University of Delaware, FY 1990 Compared with FY 2000

	FY 1990	FY 2000	% Increase
University-Administered Funds	$4,458,640	$28,036,660	528.8
State Grant Funds	$3,869,000	$6,643,500	71.7
Other Fund Sources	$2,169,602	$4,394,180	102.5
TOTAL	$10,497,242	$39,074,340	272.2

a credible data source (the American Association of University Professors magazine, *Academe*), an agreed-upon group of peer institutions, and consistent communication of information. While figure 9.3 compares 1989–90 with 1999–2000, a comparable table was provided to the campus annually, tracking progress in each fiscal year. Figure 9.3 reflects the full professor rank; comparable data was developed for other tenure-track ranks and for other categories of professional and salaried staff.

Comparable reporting to the campus community and external constituencies was essential in the area of undergraduate scholarships. Figure 9.4 compares the growth in scholarship grant funds from fiscal year 1990 to fiscal year 2000. Underscoring the differences in planning audiences, a simple total would suffice for most constituencies outside the university. After all, a 272 percent growth in ten years is quite impressive. The university gets a portion of its scholarship revenue from the State of Delaware. In making its annual request for scholarship funds, the university has

better leverage when it can demonstrate a decade-long growth of 529 percent in university-controlled funds compared with a 72 percent growth in state scholarship funds over the same period. Knowing your audiences and their information needs is essential to good planning.

The most effective way to determine the extent to which a campus has become more student centered is to ask the students. From the many commercially produced surveys that measure student satisfaction, the University of Delaware selected the ACT Student Opinion Survey. The survey measures student use of and satisfaction with twenty-three specific services (such as library, computing, academic advising, residence halls, and financial aid) and forty-three components of the campus environment (including variety and availability of courses offered, out-of-class availability of instructors, attitude of faculty and staff toward students, general registration and bill payment procedures, and quality of instructional and recreational facilities). In analyzing the data from the Student

---

Figure 9.5: Comparison of 1995 University of Delaware Scores on ACT Student Opinion Survey with 1990 Scores and with National Norms

	1990 Scores Compared with National Norms	1995 Scores Compared with 1990 Scores	1995 Scores Compared with National Norms
University Is Ahead	21	44	39
University Is Tied	14	11	15
University Is Behind	27	7	8

Opinion Survey, it is possible to compare the scores from any given administration of the instrument with prior administrations at a given institution and to compare the scores with national norms for each variable provided by ACT. Figure 9.5 examines the results from the 1995 administration of the Student Opinion Survey some four years after the student-centeredness strategic initiative was articulated campuswide. It also compares the 1995 scores with 1990 results and the national norms.

The satisfaction scores reflect a Likert scale ranging from 5 (very satisfied) to 1 (very dissatisfied). In 1995, the average university satisfaction score exceeded the national norm for comparable institutions on thirty-nine variables, compared with twenty-one in 1990. The university score lagged behind the national norm on only eight variables, compared with twenty-seven in 1990. And there were fifteen "ties" in 1995 compared with fourteen in 1990. (A tie was defined as those instances where the university score and the national norm differed by plus or minus 0.05.) While the university made significant strides in exceeding national comparators, the truly important gains were in comparison with itself. Students were more satisfied in 1995 than in 1990 on forty-four of the sixty-two variables examined, were less satisfied on only seven, and had comparable scores on eleven. This clearly demonstrated progress.

The "wins, losses, ties" analysis is yet

another example of communicating with different audiences. In developing the internal report comparing university scores with national norms, and between the 1990 and 1995 survey administrations, there was extensive discussion of statistically significant differences between scores and the confidence levels for that significance. Such a discussion is appropriate for faculty and administrators who need to understand the technical underpinning of describing differences in average scores. Such a discussion is nothing short of lethal for an audience of laypersons. On the other hand, the sports metaphor that looks at wins, losses, and ties is broadly understood and very effectively communicates the results of the assessment.

The strategic initiative to refurbish campus facilities was assessed in a number of ways. Tracking facilities expenditures and measuring the steady reduction in the backlog of deferred maintenance projects was certainly the most obvious assessment tool. The campus physical plant, when it is in pristine condition, can be an enormously effective recruiting tool. During the 1990s, the university invested heavily in new construction and in renovating and rehabilitating existing buildings and landscape. This was a strategic decision that grew out of the severe economic downturn in the region in the early part of the decade. By committing resources to capital projects at a time when construction contractors were

Figure 9.6: Student Satisfaction with Facilities

	National Norm	University of Delaware 1990	University of Delaware 1995
General condition of buildings and grounds	3.71	3.76	4.03
Athletic facilities	3.77	3.75	3.95
Availability of student housing	3.49	3.15	3.87
Classroom facilities	3.62	3.73	3.85
Study areas	3.67	3.73	3.84
Laboratory facilities	3.54	3.74	3.78

seeking work, the university was able to complete projects at substantial financial savings. As the result of this aggressive approach to facilities renewal, over 10 years the institution moved from addressing deferred maintenance to a schedule of planned maintenance. The results were also evident in student attitudes about the campus.

As we noted earlier, the ACT Student Opinion Survey utilizes a Likert scale ranging from 5 (very satisfied) to 1 (very dissatisfied). Figure 9.6 demonstrates student satisfaction scores that consistently exceed national norms at comparable institutions, but also show significant gains over 1990 satisfaction levels. The university's Office of Institutional Research and Planning has analyzed data from another survey, the Admitted Student Questionnaire, which is administered at regular intervals to all students who have been extended an offer of admission. That survey indicates that where the university is ranked as the student's second choice or lower at the time of admissions application,

when students visit the campus, in the majority of instances, they enroll at the university. Data of this sort clearly have strategic implications for the Office of Admissions, as evidenced by the robust schedule of visitation days each spring and summer.

Tactical Planning

Identifying sufficient fiscal resources to achieve competitive compensation levels, a broader funding base for undergraduate financial aid, enhanced student services, and renovation of existing campus buildings while constructing new facilities required careful tactical planning. Put simply, existing resources had to be reallocated, while new revenue streams were identified and cultivated.

Again, a specific example helps illustrate good tactical planning. We have referred to the creation of the University of Delaware's one-stop student service center previously, but offer a more extended description here. In implementing the goal for a more student-centered campus, the university faced making tactical decisions with respect to reallocation of human and fiscal resources during a severe economic downturn in the state and region. No massive infusion of new resources were available for this strategic goal. Indeed, for the goal to be realized, a complete reengineering of student services had to take place. At the direction of the university's president, the executive vice president created a steering committee comprising representatives from offices that dealt with student needs ranging from admissions, registration, and financial aid and student billing to residence life, food services, and parking permits. Students stood in long lines to register for courses in the basement of the central administration building, applied for financial aid and paid bills on the second floor of that building, crossed campus in one direction to obtain a meal plan, in another direction to obtain a student identification card, and yet another direction to obtain a parking permit.

While falling under the general umbrella of student services, these offices reported to disparate vice presidents and constituted anything but a seamless web of services for student consumers. The members of the steering committee were told to forget their reporting lines and think of themselves as students while designing a student services delivery system that would be responsive to student needs rather than administrative convenience.

At the time that the steering committee

was doing its tactical planning, opportunities were identified that would directly affect the delivery of student services:

- A building on the central campus that had formerly been occupied by a start-up business became available. For approximately $1 million, the facility could be rehabilitated and renovated to provide a central location for student services.

- The university had been investing over the past several years in online computing technology. This technology could now be used to allow student self-service to register for courses, order transcripts, monitor progress in fulfilling degree requirements, and other functions that had previously required interaction with professional and clerical staff.

The steering committee arrived at a series of recommendations for restructuring the delivery of student services that took advantage of both of these opportunities. The renovated industrial building would become the new Student Services Building, which would be configured to maximize the ease with which student needs and inquiries would be addressed. Specifically, the building and associated staff would be structured as follows:

- The overriding objective within the Student Services Building would be to have a student's needs met by having that student interact with no more than one staff member or, in appropriate circumstances, no staff at all through self-service such as online query tools. To that end, the Student Services Building was staffed with a cadre of well-trained generalist personnel capable of responding to questions related to all fields of student services, including admissions, registration, financial aid, student billing, residence life, food services, and parking.

- A smaller group of specialist personnel representing these functional areas would be available to answer questions of sufficient complexity where a generalist response would not suffice.

- The Student Services Building would be equipped with a bank of computer kiosks that would allow student access to a variety of products that, heretofore, required assistance from a staff member. These products included student schedules, student grade reports, unofficial transcripts, and degree audits.

Student access via computer to these sorts of products is now old hat at most institutions, including the University of Delaware, where personal computers now provide similar access from dormitory rooms, off-campus residences, or anywhere in the world via the Internet. However, in the early 1990s this concept of "one-stop shopping" was revolutionary. Students were suddenly largely self-sufficient in accessing the

student services information they needed. And where interaction with a university employee was required, staff were trained in customer relations sensitivity, training that student services staff lacked in years past. The student satisfaction scores in figure 9.6 contrast the pre-Student Services Building era (1990 and before) with the post-Student Services Building era (1995 and after).

While the implementation of processes and measures for achieving the goal of a more student-centered campus was important, other benefits accrued from the tactical decisions that were made. By taking advantage of technology in implementing the new Student Services Building, the university was able to eliminate positions. The elimination of positions was largely accomplished by not appointing a replacement upon the retirement or resignation of an incumbent and through retraining and redeployment of existing personnel to vacant positions in other areas of the university. The savings associated with the reduction of student services positions freed up recurring salary and benefits dollars for reallocation to other institutional needs, most notably the competitive compensation and scholarship strategic goals.

Funding the other strategic goals required other tactical decisions. The university is a relatively tuition-dependent institution, with roughly 45 percent of its education and general expenditures covered by tuition revenue. In determining how to fund the four strategic initiatives, it was clear that it could not be done through inordinate tuition increases. The university is committed to a policy of, where possible, holding annual tuition increases close to the inflation rate, thereby allowing students and parents a predictable estimate of what a university education will cost from year to year. Moreover, one of the strategic initiatives focused on enhanced student access through increased scholarship aid. It would be counterproductive to that goal to allow extraordinary tuition increases.

The decision to hold tuition increases close to the level of inflation obviated the next set of tactical decisions related to implementation of the strategic goals— the university's existing revenue streams had to be diversified. Two candidates, in particular, became focal points— externally funded contracts and grants, and gifts.

Research universities generally do not view research activity as a money maker, as the funds associated with contracts and grants are restricted in their use. However, recovery of indirect costs associated with that research activity does provide an avenue for funneling funds into the general institutional revenue stream, and for an institution with a modest base of external funds activities, growing that base significantly represents a real opportunity. In 1991, when the university initially articulated the strategic initiatives, externally funded contracts and grants expenditures

totaled $47.8 million; by 1995 these had grown to $61 million, and by the end of the decade they were $94.2 million, effectively doubling that income stream in less than ten years. In addition to supporting pure and applied research at the university, this expansion of externally funded scholarship generated significantly greater tuition and stipend support for graduate students.

While gifts to an institution also tend to be restricted in their uses, institutions can request that those gifts be targeted for specific purposes during capital campaigns. Donors are generally quite happy to have their gifts become part of endowment funds, the income from which is restricted to providing undergraduate scholarships. This use is wholly consistent with the strategic goals at the University of Delaware. Gifts to the university totaled $17 million in 1991; the annual total increased to $21 million in 1995 and reached $42.6 million in 2000, an increase of 150 percent in less than a decade.

The University of Delaware is fortunate to have a sizeable endowment, and the income from it contributes to the operating budget as an unrestricted revenue stream. Growing that endowment, however, requires tactical planning with respect to how funds are invested. The university's Board of Trustees has a strict policy that limits the annual income from the endowment that may be expended so that in most years sufficient income is retained in the endowment to offset inflation. In 1991, the university endowment totaled $356.2 million; by 1995, it had grown to $435.1 million. The university prospered in the economic climate of the 1990s, and by the end of the decade, the endowment had grown to $928.4 million and stands in excess of $1 billion today, the return from which has contributed to institutional strategic goals and objectives.

It should be quite evident from this discussion that planning for the articulation of both long-range and strategic goals and objectives, while critical to the overall planning process, is not sufficient. It must be accompanied by tactical planning that provides for decisions such as the deployment of appropriate human and fiscal resources to achieve goals and objectives.

Over the past fifteen years, the University of Delaware has consciously incorporated strategic planning and outcomes assessment into the fabric of university life. The Office of Institutional Research and Planning and the Budget Office created analytical and reporting structures in the early 1990s that were intended to guide the institution through a difficult fiscal situation wherein millions of dollars in recurring budgetary items had to be moved from nonrecurring revenue sources. Having balanced the budget, those analytical and reporting tools remain in place to this day to ensure efficient and economical use of fiscal resources at the department

and unit level. Where balancing the budget was the focus nearly two decades ago, the current focus is the allocation and reallocation of limited resources in support of current and new initiatives. Obviously, tough decisions continue to be made during resource reallocation— some units become "winners" and others "losers," and it is imperative to have accessible and broadly understood analytical/assessment data to support such decisions.

Where the university outcomes data regarding employee compensation levels, financial aid allocations, student satisfaction studies, and physical plant renovation show the gains described in this chapter, it is crucial to continue those sorts of assessments to ensure that gains are not squandered.

Planning and assessment have become an integral part of university thinking. While the University of Delaware, like most institutions, struggles from time to time with policy development and new initiatives, the struggles are substantially ameliorated through a clearly understood, participatory planning process in which decisions are rooted in multiple measures of outcomes data.

Chapter 10

Building Planning and Assessment Processes on Your Campus

Constructing a planning process is not formulaic—there is no one-size-fits-all template for building an integrated planning and assessment process into the institutional culture of a specific college or university. However, it is possible to bring together a summary of ideas and suggestions that may offer some assistance in the development and implementation of integrated processes.

Taken together, the authors possess a cumulative total of about a century of experience in college and university planning. Based on our experiences, we know that the need for and the challenges of planning and assessment are changing. It is no longer enough to have an institutional plan or to show that some attention is being paid to assessment. Good planning processes really must include linkages to sustained analysis and assessment for judgments to be made about progress toward goals and objectives.

Development of planning and assessment capabilities should be viewed as a journey rather than a destination. The results from one iteration of planning and assessment should lead naturally to a new iteration of the process. Our best advice is to focus on what is useful and sustainable within the specific circumstances of the institution. The following list of "helpful hints" is intended to assist readers in thinking about the integration of planning and assessment.

Helpful Hints: Assuring Successful Integration of Planning and Assessment

Starting from Institutional Mission

A current, accurate, and complete mission statement is a fundamental prerequisite for good planning and assessment. The mission statement should define the institution, clearly communicate the businesses it will engage in, and convey a sense of its unique character. Just as author George Keller cautioned against allowing platitudes to permeate a plan (see chapter 2), institutions should guard against such ill-founded ideas permeating a mission statement. The mission should serve as a firm foundation for the institutional decisions and choices that are contained in its plans.

Missions do change and evolve over time, however, and it is important that provision be made to return periodically and systematically to a consideration of the mission. This may be accomplished, for example, by making mission review an early part of a new planning cycle.

Understanding the Market and Creating a "Brand"

Market and branding decisions should naturally follow from and represent an extension of the mission of the institution. Once an institution knows the basic markets it wishes to serve, it should direct its attention to establishing and maintaining a recognizable brand. This may sound far too commercial for many in higher education today, but the work, if not the language, is already present. Consider, for example, the admissions view books that typically are produced for prospective freshmen. What are these if not a means of explaining the institutional brand?

To be avoided is any temptation to rush into new markets that appear to represent a quick and easy means of increasing revenue streams. Without careful planning, a rush to new markets might bring unintended consequences and costs that could be greater than the benefits derived from the new market. A recent example of this phenomenon is the decision of a number of U. S. institutions to move into international markets. To offer international programs successfully, an institution, at a minimum, must understand the culture and be able to negotiate the demands of licensure/regulation that may apply in the country of operation.

Covering Long-Range, Strategic, Tactical, and Operational Plans and Decisions

There is no universally agreed-upon taxonomy of planning, and terms may be used somewhat differently from institution to institution. Whatever the language used, however, it is important

that attention be paid to decisions that address various time horizons and purposes. And, once again, all of these decisions should be rooted in the institutional mission.

Long-term and strategic plans should set the stage, articulating directions chosen and specific strategies that will help the institution achieve its mission. Decisions represented in these types of plans typically are focused most on "what" an institution does. Tactical and operational plans usually address a shorter time frame and are more about "how" to achieve the purposes of the institution.

It is also important to acknowledge that many aspects of planning represent an art form rather than a science. For example, in establishing plans, it is necessary to decide exactly how bold the goals should be. Are the institution and its constituencies ready to address difficult goals that require an ability to stretch? Or would it be better at a specific time in the life of a particular institution to establish more modest goals that will allow for development of a record of success?

Integrating Academic, Resource, and Facilities Elements

In chapter 3, we expressed our belief that academic planning is the engine that should drive other types of planning. Academic planning springs from the unique mission of the institution and identifies the current program and services choices that have been made. However, we have also noted our belief in a holistic notion of planning—that program and service choices must be appropriately supported through decisions regarding resources (e.g., human resources, budgets, fund-raising, and investments) and facilities (e.g., renewal/replacement of buildings, campus infrastructure, and technology). Although it may be important to work independently in each functional area, it is also important, for the sake of efficiency, that there be a concern for the overall consistency of decision making.

Deciding What's Important, Setting Priorities, and Establishing a Timetable

Deciding what's important, setting priorities, and establishing a timetable are all elements of the planning process that require finesse. Such decisions are best made when "the art of the possible" is taken into consideration for the specific institution.

Anyone who has engaged in the process of developing a plan knows how easy it is to come up with lots of good ideas. What's not possible is to do all things well at the same time. Culling lists of good ideas, deciding what's important, and setting priorities are crucial in establishing a sound plan. The tendency to try to do too many different things is perhaps greatest when an institution is new to the planning process, but all institutions need to remain aware of this potential planning pitfall. It should be self-evident that the chances of success are greater when effort is concentrated on a reasonable number of the most important projects.

Once a list of the most important goals has been established, it is important that a realistic timetable be constructed. The tendency to require immediate action on all things in the plan should be avoided. It is important to pace the work so that burn-out does not become a factor, but regular progress is sustained.

Using Plans as Guidelines for Action Rather Than Documents Set in Stone

An institutional plan should not be viewed as something set in stone for the time period specified. Rather, it should be a guide that identifies important goals as well as other relevant information. In the category of other relevant information are items such as the individuals responsible, reasonable timetables for project completion, and resources that may be required.

Although a plan may be an important document, it exists in a dynamic environment. Change is constant. As the environment (internal as well as external) changes, modifications and adjustments in either goals or the course employed to achieve a goal may be necessary.

At the end of the day, the plan itself may be much less important than the planning process. The process, at its best, represents the means whereby people come together to think through what is and what should be at an institution.

Identifying and Implementing Appropriate Linkage Points

Throughout this volume, we have clearly advocated linking the planning and assessment processes. In practice, how is this done? One of the most practical ways to achieve the desired result may be to seek out those points where it makes best sense to ensure that the results of one process are effectively linked into other processes. An example of how not to achieve the desired integration is found where planning, assessment, and resource allocation have matured as separate and completely independent processes that run on independent and incompatible timetables. To correct the situation, it may be beneficial to ask questions such as the following: When are significant assessment results or milestones known? Can results from assessments be scheduled so that there can be an impact on the annual budget decision-making processes? How can assessments be best scheduled so that results may be built into successive rounds of institutional planning?

Integrating Assessments, Plans, and Budgets

The previous section makes it clear that we believe that it is, in fact, important to go beyond integrating planning and assessment to include budgets. Plans identify what an institution is attempting to accomplish. Assessments allow the institution to judge whether it is achieving its goals. Budgets make it clear that the institution is willing and able to allocate necessary resources to achieve those purposes and projects that are deemed most essential for the present and future of the institution. While planning, like assessment, requires creativity and imagination, it may be the case that even more creativity and imagination will be required to find ways to fund what should and perhaps must be done to assure a productive future.

Acknowledging the Leadership Imperative

The importance of institutional leadership is well chronicled elsewhere in the literature of higher education, and we have not attempted to duplicate it here. It is important, however, to note the critical need for leadership in the areas we have discussed in this book. We maintain that it is not possible to have meaningful integrated planning and assessment without institutional leadership that understands the value in these processes and supports the work that must be done. That is clearly evident in the presidential leadership that drove events in the University of Delaware case study (see chapter 9).

To achieve usefully integrated planning and assessment, institutional leaders may need to become champions of the cause. Leaders regularly make decisions about how institutional resources will be employed. Making certain that adequate time and human resources are applied to the process and that results are used for institutional improvements are some of the things that leaders can do to signal the importance of linked planning and assessment. Sending clear signals about such things may be particularly important when an institution is newly engaged in developing a culture of planning and assessment.

Achieving Broad Participation and Wide Communication

Much of the existing literature on planning speaks to the value of broad participation and wide communication in planning. It is important that constituencies have a voice as plans are developed even though it is not possible for a good plan to reflect the favored goals of all groups. In a meaningful participative process, all of the constituencies are heard and understandings are developed and shared regarding the selection of important goals.

Achieving broad participation and wide communication is not trivial. Managing a participative process and assuring full communication is labor intensive. In our experience, however, the effort is always worth the associated costs in time and energy. Teamwork is necessary to achieve goals, and good teamwork starts with meaningful participation and good communication.

Understanding the Value of a Decision Model

Some institutions may find that it is useful to investigate and perhaps adopt a decision-making process or model. A conscious decision of this nature may

be particularly important and helpful where planning and assessment are not routine parts of the institutional culture and where the institution is attempting to develop or reengineer linked planning and assessment processes. Reviewing one or more decision models may help an institution understand how processes can flow and where linkage points may be appropriate. The most frequently cited decision/process model in use today is probably the Baldrige approach, but there are many others as well.

It should be understood that we are not advocates of a particular decision-making or process model. What we do advocate, however, is careful attention to processes to assure that these remain useful and beneficial to the institution.

Developing and Implementing an Active and Continuing Process

In our experience, a common and useful approach to integration of planning, assessment and other processes such as budgeting is to have a central steering committee or committees that oversee, synthesize, and manage. The steering committee may make use of subcommittees. A few cautions about the nature of planning and budget steering committees are in order. While participatory planning is essential to consensus on major issues, it is important to avoid creating committees and subcommittees that are so large and cumbersome that little, if anything, gets accomplished. Clear delineation of roles and responsibilities is essential.

A steering committee tends to be a quasi-permanent fixture, overseeing the planning process over time. Subcommittees, on the other hand, report their work to the steering committee and then disappear, with new subcommittees arising as new planning issues and initiatives surface.

Staffing an Integrated Planning/Assessment/Budget Process

Staffing a planning process correctly is essential to success. Certain key players must be at the table. While the president of a college or university frequently has insufficient time to chair or be a participating member of a steering committee, the chief academic officer and the chief administrative officer should either engage the steering committee themselves or appoint senior-level designees to represent them. Faculty representation is essential, often in the person of the president of the faculty senate or other representatives from faculty governance groups. At those campuses where faculty is unionized, we discourage inclusion of faculty as representatives of their union because their function is negotiation of terms and conditions of employment, not institutional vision, direction, and policy. Finally, while student participation in planning is important, it can be accomplished in a variety of ways. For example, students might be more effective participants at the subcommittee level in recognition of the fact that student populations are transient, while the planning process

should be enduring.

Appropriate staff support for integrated processes is also essential. Since assessment of institutional effectiveness and outcomes is a critical component of measuring the success of planning initiatives, quantitative and qualitative analytical expertise must be brought to bear in support of the planning process. Usually, the necessary expertise for analysis can be found in offices of institutional research and in offices dedicated to assessment functions. To ensure that planning is reality based, it is also important to have a campus budget officer available as a regular contributing member of integrated processes. We have seen countless elaborate planning documents that have no relationship to campus resource allocation. How and on which functions resources are expended is the clearest indication of what an institution's priorities are. Planning and budgeting are inextricably interrelated, and a clear linkage between planning and budgeting must be evident.

Learning What Others Are Doing

Benchmarking and best practice information is essential in today's competitive higher education environment. Such information is readily available from numerous sources and is equally applicable in content and process areas.

This type of research helps an institution make good decisions. However, it should be recognized that such efforts do have associated costs. It takes time to do the research and complete useful analyses, and it may be necessary that some staff have technical expertise in relevant areas.

Sometimes, a group of institutions can work together to share a common vision as well as technical planning and assessment resources. The New Jersey Higher Education Partnership for Sustainability has a shared vision that includes the measurement and reduction of energy consumption and greenhouse gas emissions. Participants share analytical tools and have built a joint partnership with state government.

Obtaining and Using Expert Advice and Assistance

Individual consultants or consulting firms may be an excellent resource when an institution requires specialized assistance and expertise that is not readily available in-house. For example, colleges and universities frequently engage an outside firm to develop a campus master plan to access the services of a number of people with specialized knowledge and experience. The same needs lead an institution to engage a firm to provide assistance with other projects, such as development of a strategic plan/process or development an outcomes assessment plan/process.

Developing the Capacity for Assessment and Institutional Research

It is becoming increasingly apparent that the prospect for successful planning and assessment is enhanced where a college or university has a formal

institutional research function. Analytical responsibilities that are housed in offices other than institutional research, e.g., a registrar's or admissions office, are frequently secondary to the central mission of such offices. As a result, the institution may not have the benefit of the kind of analytical, evidence-based information that can support effective planning, assessment, and decision making.

An institutional research office can serve as a focal point for production of the kind of analytical, evidence-based information just mentioned. An office of this type plays an important role in data collection and can assume some responsibility for the institution's archive of vital statistics and information. More importantly, however, it plays a central role in analyzing data and interpreting results. Additionally, institutional research staff may share expertise with other academic and administrative units.

While institutional research may represent an investment in terms of designated personnel, office space, and budget, the investment may provide valuable rewards in the form of information about where the institution is and where it is headed.

Judging Progress and Recalibrating the Plan

"How are we doing?" This is a question, whether actually asked or only implied, that regularly plays in the background where planning and assessment have become part of the institutional culture.

In such places, good news and not-so-good news are equally valued. Good news about progress toward achieving goals outlined in the plan is celebrated. The not-so-good news provides information about areas where additional efforts may be required.

In some instances, it may become clear that the goals contained in the plan were not what they should have been. Goals might be too difficult to achieve or too easily achieved. One example of this is found in the development area with regard to plans for capital campaigns. As a campaign progresses, it will become clear whether the established goals were reasonable. If targets were too difficult to achieve, an explanation or reasons for the lack of success will be explored and new, more realistic targets will be established. If this recalibration is necessary, it may also be essential to alter other expectations. For example, if a capital campaign does not generate all of the gift revenue expected, it may be necessary to cut back in those places where the institution anticipated using the new resources.

We should make it clear, however, that we do not advocate changing the plan on a continuous basis. As we noted previously, a plan should be exactly that. While we acknowledge that there is a natural tendency to want to achieve success, we caution against obsessive or compulsive behavior regarding the goals in the plan. An institution will get better at establishing correct and achievable goals as it gains experience through several iterations of the planning process. Further, we believe that available energies should be directed toward fulfilling goals rather than constantly reworking them.

Periodically Evaluating the Integrated Planning and Assessment Processes

Establishing an integrated set of planning and assessment processes is difficult and labor intensive, and there may be an understandable tendency to underestimate the work and attention required to keep the whole on track and relevant to the ongoing life of the institution. One way of assuring that processes remain fresh and useful is to take the time to assess the processes themselves periodically. Are the right people involved? Are the right questions being asked? Are results useful in thinking about and working on institutional improvements? Are results from various parts of the planning and assessment processes being used appropriately?

Closing Thoughts

As we noted in the Preface, our intention is not to provide a cookbook approach to planning, but to provide a conceptual framework to enable institutions to identify the essential and relevant elements of good planning and assessment, and to customize those elements to fit the culture and environment in which they operate. We hope that readers will find that we have been successful in providing practical examples and guidance.

In chapter 2, we highlighted George Keller's assessment of what constitutes good strategic planning. It is worthwhile to restate those assessments:

- Strategy making is a blend of rational and economic analysis, political maneuvering, and psychological interplay. It is therefore participatory and highly tolerant of controversy.

- Strategic planning concentrates on the fate of the institution above everything else.

- Academic strategic decision making means that a college, school, or university and its leaders are active rather than passive about their position in history.

- Strategic planning looks outward and is focused on keeping the institution in step with the changing environment.

- Academic strategy making is competitive, recognizing that higher education is subject to economic market conditions and to increasingly strong competition.

- Strategic planning concentrates on decisions, not on documented plans, analyses, forecasts, and goals.[50]

The discussion and examples throughout this volume are intended to reinforce Keller's notion that planning is not a static activity, but a vital and proactive process intended to keep a college or university in step with its ever-changing environment, while at the same time pursuing strategies that lead toward a fuller realization of its core mission.

This publication concludes with a resource guide and a selected bibliography. These references are intended as additional tools that will allow you to sample ideas and practices developed and applied in a variety of settings.

50. George Keller, *Academic Strategy: the Management Revolution in American Higher Education* (Baltimore: Johns Hopkins University Press, 1983), 143–50.

Bibliography and Other Selected Resources

A Note About the Bibliography

This bibliography is intended to highlight resources that we specifically consulted for this publication and to direct the reader to works and sources that might be of continuing interest. Our intent is the production of a practical guide, and we believe that an extended list of resource options is useful. We hope that the information contained here will assist readers who are investigating ways to improve linkages and connections among planning, assessment, and resource allocation.

Higher Education Associations

Many major associations represent various sectors of higher education (e.g., the American Association of State Colleges and Universities, the National Association of State Universities and Land-Grant Colleges, the Council of Independent Colleges, and the American Association of Community Colleges). Other associations represent various functions within higher education (e.g., the American Association of Collegiate Registrars and Admissions Officers and the American Association of University Professors). Our intent with the limited listing that follows is to highlight those associations that most frequently contribute to the knowledge base concerning the practice of integrated planning and assessment by colleges and universities.

The American Council on Education (www.acenet.edu) serves as a centralized voice and leadership/representational organization for higher education. Especially valuable is the interactive library resources available via the Web.

The Association of Governing Boards of Universities and Colleges (www.agb.org) is a national organization dedicated to providing public and private college and university presidents and boards of trustees with resources to enhance their effectiveness.

The Association for Institutional Research (www.airweb.org) is the professional association representing institutional research personnel at colleges and universities. The focus of many of this organization's publications is on practical approaches for research, data collection, and analysis.

The Association for the Advancement of Sustainability in Higher Education (www.aashe.org) is a national organization helping colleges and universities to include sustainability in all aspects of their operations through education, communication, research, and professional development.

The Council for Higher Education Accreditation (www.chea.org) is a private, nonprofit national organization that coordinates accreditation activity in the United States.

The National Association of College and University Business Officers (www.nacubo.org) represents chief administrative and financial officers of colleges, universities, and education service providers.

The Society for College and University Planning (www.scup.org) is an association focused on the promotion, advancement, and application of effective planning in all functional areas of higher education. Of particular note for SCUP members is the library of Web site linkages to several hundred plans that have been developed by various colleges and universities.

Regional Accreditors

The Web sites of the U.S. regional accreditation agencies for higher education are listed below. These sites include information about accreditation standards used by each association as well as information about other publications and professional development opportunities available through each agency.

Middle States Commission on Higher Education
www.msche.org

New England Association of Schools and Colleges
www.neasc.org

North Central Association of Colleges and Schools
www.ncahigherlearningcommission.org

Northwest Commission on Colleges and Universities
www.nwccu.org

Southern Association of Colleges and Schools
www.sacs.org

Western Association of Colleges and Schools
www.wascweb.org

Higher Education Journals

Listed below are a few of the higher education journals that we have found, over the years, to include a number of timely and useful articles about practical aspects of planning and assessment as well as about linking planning, assessment, and resource allocation decisions.

Assessment Update. San Francisco: Jossey-Bass.

Business Officer. Washington, DC: National Association of College and University Business Officers.

Change. Washington, DC: Heldref Publications.

New Directions for Community Colleges. San Francisco: Jossey-Bass,.

New Directions for Higher Education. San Francisco: Jossey-Bass.

New Directions for Institutional Research. San Francisco: Jossey-Bass.

Planning for Higher Education. Ann Arbor, MI: Society for College and University Planning.

Books Referenced in This Publication

Accrediting Commission for Senior Colleges and Universities, Western Association of Schools and Colleges. Handbook of Accreditation. Alameda, CA: Western Association of Schools and Colleges, 2001.

Commission on Colleges, Southern Association of Colleges and Schools. *Principles of Accreditation: Foundations for Quality Enhancement*. Decatur, GA: Commission on Colleges, Southern Association of Colleges and Schools, 2001.

Commission on Institutions of Higher Education. *Standards for Accreditation*. Bedford, MA: Commission on Institutions of Higher Education, 2005.

The Higher Learning Commission. *The Handbook of Accreditation*. Version 1:10/03. Chicago: The Higher Learning Commission, 2003.

Keller, George. *Academic Strategy: The Management Revolution in American Higher Education*. Baltimore: Johns Hopkins University Press, 1983.

Middle States Commission on Higher Education. *Characteristics of Excellence in Higher Education: Eligibility Requirements and Standards for Accreditation*. Philadelphia: Middle States Commission on Higher Education, 2006.

Norris, Donald M., and Nick L. Poulton. *A Guide for New Planners*. Ann Arbor, MI: Society for College and University Planning, 1991.

Prager, Sealy & Co., LLC; KPMG LLP; and BearingPoint, Inc. *Strategic Financial Analysis for Higher Education* (Sixth Edition). Washington, D.C.: National Association of College and University Business Officers, 2005.

Turk, F.J., and F.J. Praeger. *Ratio Analysis in Higher Education: Measuring Past Performance to Chart Direction*. Washington, DC: National Association of College and University Business Officers, 1999.

Web Site Resources Referenced in This Publication

Note that all Web site references are current as of the preparation of this list; however, the content and location of information on the World Wide Web is fluid and may have changed in the interim.

ACT, Inc. Information about the College Student Needs Assessment Survey, including details about separate versions for four-year and two-year institutions. www.act.org.

Anthony W. Marx, remarks at his inauguration as president of Amherst College, Amherst, MA, October 26, 2003. www.amherst.edu/news/inauguration/address.html.

_____. Profile of the class of 2008 found in the Fifty-Eighth Annual Report to Secondary Schools. www.amherst.edu/admission/process/ssr08.pdf.

_____. Description of tutorial and academic writing services. From the World Wide Web: www.amherst.edu/~dos/acadsupport.html.

Baldrige National Quality Program. Description of the program designed to enhance quality and productivity of U.S. organizations including higher education. From the World Wide Web: www.quality.nist.gov/.

California State University Northridge, Northridge, CA. Values Statement. From the World Wide Web: www.csun.edu/academic.affairs/csunmission.htm.

Delaware Valley College, Doylestown, PA. Profile of the class of 2007. From the World Wide Web: www.devalcol.edu/services/research/downloads/profiles/2003.pdf.

_____. Description of the CHOICES program offered through Counseling and Learning Support Services. From the World Wide Web: www.devalcol.edu/academics/counseling/services_choices.html.

_____. Description of the Higher Education Equal Opportunity Program (ACT 101). From the World Wide Web: www.devalcol.edu/academics/counseling/services_act101.html.

Duke University, Durham, NC. Mission Statement approved by the Board of Trustees October 1, 1994; revised February 23, 2001. From the World Wide Web: www.planning.duke.edu/mission.html.

Hoover's, Inc., Austin TX. Description of the Apollo Group and the University of Phoenix. From the World Wide Web: www.hoovers.com/apollo-group?--ID__42338--/free-co-factsheet.xhtml.

Iowa State University, Ames, IA. Mission Statement and Role Statement. From the

World Wide Web: www.iastate.edu/about/.

Johnson County Community College, Overland Park, KS. From the World Wide Web: www.jccc.net/home/site/welcome/tocaboutjccc/missionall

_____. Kansas Study of Instructional Costs and Productivity. From the World Wide Web: www.kansasstudy.org.

_____. National Community College Benchmarking Project. From the World Wide Web: www.nccbp.org.

National Center for Education Statistics, Washington, D.C. Information about the Postsecondary Education Facilities Inventory and Classification Manual. From the World Wide Web: www.nces.ed.gov/pubs92/92165.pdf.

Northwestern Connecticut Community College, Winstead, CT. Mission Statement. From the World Wide Web: www.nwcc.commnet.edu.

Noel-Levitz, Inc. Description of instrumentation for various higher education sectors. From the World Wide Web: www.noellevitz.com.

Reed College, Portland, OR. Description of the college. From the World Wide Web: web.reed.edu/apply/reed_history.html.

Rhodes College, Memphis, TN. Vision Statement. From the World Wide Web: www.rhodes.edu/AboutRhodes/RhodesVision/index.cfm.

Society for College and University Planning, Ann Arbor, MI. Campus Master Planning Documents. From the World Wide Web: www.scup.org/knowledge/campus_plans.html.

Temple University, Philadelphia, PA. Mission of the Student Activities Department. From the World Wide Web: www.temple.edu/SAC/index2.html.

_____. Description of the Learning Communities at Temple University. From the World Wide Web: www.temple.edu/LC/lc_students.html.

The College of New Jersey, Trenton, NJ. History of The College of New Jersey. From the World Wide Web: www.tcnj.edu/%7Eccr/about/history.html.

University of Delaware, Newark, DE. Delaware Study of Instructional Costs and Productivity. From the World Wide Web: www.udel.edu/ir/cost.

_____. Description of the Learning Integrated Freshman Experience (LIFE). From the World Wide Web: life.ugs.udel.edu//.

_____. Description of Special Interest Housing at the University of Delaware.

From the World Wide Web: www.udel.edu/reslife/students/sih.html.

_____. Description of the teaching emphasis at the University of Delaware. From the World Wide Web: www.udel.edu/admissions/viewbook/explore/teachers.html.

_____. Report to the Faculty Senate: Academic Progress at the University of Delaware, February 2005. From the World Wide Web: www.udel.edu/provost/AcademicProgress.pdf.

University of Massachusetts at Boston, Boston, MA. Fact sheet information. From the World Wide Web: www.umb.edu/faculty_staff/ir/2004/facts.html.

University of Phoenix, Phoenix, AZ. Description of the University of Phoenix, a university for working adults. From the World Wide Web: www.phoenix.edu.

West Chester University, West Chester, PA. Vision and Mission Statements. From the World Wide Web: www.wcupa.edu/.

Selected Benchmarking Resources

The following list of selected benchmarking resources is intended to provide some initial ideas that the reader may wish to explore. This listing is not intended to be comprehensive or exhaustive.

ACT. This organization offers more than a dozen standardized survey instruments, some of which are specific either to two-year or four-year institutions, for use in higher education. Included among the various surveys are (1) the College Student Needs Assessment Survey, focusing on perceived personal and educational needs of students, (2) the Student Opinion Survey, which is designed to address student satisfaction with programs, services, and other aspects of the college experience, and (3) the Survey of Student Opinions, which centers on student perceptions of and satisfaction with programs, services, and environmental factors at the institution attended. The ACT Web site is www.act.org.

American Association of University Professors (AAUP). Results of an annual survey of faculty salaries and compensation are reported annually in the March–April issue of Academe, the AAUP magazine. Information about the survey can also be accessed through the AAUP Web site at www.aaup.org.

The Association of Research Libraries (ARL) collects information about academic library performance measures and statistics. Information about the ARL surveys can be found on the association's Web site at www.arl.org/stats.

The College Board. This organization offers the Admitted Student Questionnaire, a survey that asks respondents about perceptions of programs, services, and marketing for a specific institution as compared with others. This resource can be accessed through the College Board Web site at www.collegeboard.com.

College & University Professional Association for Human Resources (CUPA-HR). CUPA-HR conducts annual studies of salaries and compensation covering faculty and administrative categories. Information about the annual surveys can be accessed via the organization's Web site at www.cupahr.org/surveys.

The National Center for Education Statistics (NCES). Through the Integrated Postsecondary Education Data System (IPEDS), NCES collects a wide variety of data from colleges and universities, including information about institutional characteristics, enrollment, completions and graduation rates, instructional faculty, finances, financial aid, and staff. Information about the surveys and results that can be downloaded is available at nces.ed.gov/ipeds.

National Survey of Student Engagement (NSSE) and the Community College Survey of Student Engagement. The NSSE was the first of several surveys designed to collect information about student participation in programs and activities provided by institutions for student learning and development. Variations of the survey are now available for community colleges, four-year institutions, and law schools. These surveys may be accessed at nsse.iub.edu.

Society for College and University Planning (SCUP). A wide variety of institutional plans are available through the SCUP Web site at www.scup.org/knowledge/campus_plans.html.

University of Delaware. The Delaware Study of Instructional Costs and Productivity provides participants with detailed information about teaching loads, instructional costs, and externally funded scholarship. The Web site for this study is found at www.udel.edu/ir/cost.

Other Publications of Potential Interest to Readers

Astin, Alexander W. *Assessment for Excellence: The Philosophy and Practice of Assessment and Evaluation in Higher Education*. Portland: Oryx and American Council on Education, 1991.

Alstete, Jeffrey W. *Accreditation Matters: Achieving Academic Recognition and Renewal*. ASHE Higher Education Report, vol. 30, no. 4. San Francisco: Jossey-Bass, 2004.

————. *Benchmarking in Higher Education: Adapting Best Practices to Improve Quality*. San Francisco: Jossey-Bass, 1996.

Ammentorp, Bill, and Bill Warner. *Academic Design: Sharing Lessons Learned*. Ann Arbor, MI: Society for College and University Planning, 2003.

Angelo, Thomas A., and K. Patricia Cross. *Classroom Assessment Techniques: A Handbook for College Teachers*. 2nd ed. San Francisco: Jossey-Bass, 1993.

Balderston, Frederick E. *Managing Today's University: Strategies for Viability, Change, and Excellence*. 2nd ed. San Francisco: Jossey-Bass, 1995.

Banta, Trudy W., Jon P. Lund, Karen E. Black, and Frances W. Oblander. *Assessment in Practice: Putting Principles to Work on College Campuses*. San Francisco: Jossey-Bass, 1995.

Bender, Barbara E., and John H. Schuh, eds. *Using Benchmarking to Inform Practice in Higher Education*. New Directions for Higher Education, no. 118. San Francisco: Jossey-Bass, 2002.

Birnbaum, Robert. *Management Fads in Higher Education: Where They Came From, What They Do, Why They Fail*. San Francisco: Jossey-Bass, 2000.

Bok, Derek. *Universities in the Marketplace*. Princeton: Princeton University Press, 2003.

Borden, Victor M.H., and Jody L. Zak. *Measuring Quality: Choosing Among Surveys and Other Assessments of College Quality*. Washington, DC: American Council on Education; Tallahassee: Association for Institutional Research, 2001.

Bowen, William G., and Harold T. Shapiro. *Universities and Their Leadership*. Princeton: Princeton University Press, 1998.

Bryson, John M. *Strategic Planning for Public and Nonprofit Organizations: A Guide to Strengthening and Sustaining Organizational Achievement*. 3rd ed. San Francisco: Jossey-Bass, 2004.

Burke, Joseph C., ed. *Achieving Accountability in Higher Education: Balancing Public, Academic, and Market Demands*. San Francisco: Jossey-Bass, 2004.

Dew, John Robert, and Molly McGowan Nearing. *Continuous Quality Improvement in Higher Education*. Westport, CT: American Council on Education/Praeger, 2004.

Dickmeyer, Nathan. *The Strategic Attitude: Integrating Strategic Planning into Daily University Worklife*. Washington, DC: National Association of College and University Business Officers, 2004.

Dolence, Michael G., Daniel James Rowley, and Herman D. Lujan. *Working Toward Strategic Change: A Step-by-Step Guide to the Planning Process*. San Francisco: Jossey-Bass, 1997.

Dooris, Michael, John Kelley, and James F. Trainer. *Successful Strategic Planning. New Directions for Institutional Research, no. 123*. San Francisco: Jossey-Bass, 2004.

Gaither, Gerald H., Brian P. Nedwek, and John E. Neal. *Measuring Up: The Promises and Pitfalls of Performance Indicators in Higher Education*. San Francisco: Jossey-Bass, 1994.

Gardiner, Lion F., Caitlin Anderson, and Barbara L. Cambridge, eds. *Learning Through Assessment: A Resource Guide for Higher Education*. Washington, DC: American Association for Higher Education, 1997.

Huba, Mary E., and Jann E. Freed. *Learner-Centered Assessment on College Campuses: Shifting the Focus from Teaching to Learning*. Boston: Allyn and Bacon, 2000.

Johnson, Sandra L., Sean C. Rush, eds. *Reinventing the University: Managing and Financing Institutions of Higher Education*. New York: John Wiley & Sons, Inc., 1995.

Kotter, John P. *Leading Change*. Boston: Harvard Business School Press, 1996.

Leslie, David W., and E. K. Fretwell, Jr. *Wise Moves in Hard Times: Creating and Managing Resilient Colleges and Universities*. San Francisco: Jossey-Bass, 1996.

Martin, James, James E. Samels, and Associates. *First Among Equals: The Role of the Chief Academic Officer*. Baltimore: The Johns Hopkins University Press, 2000.

McPherson, Michael S., Morton Owen Schapiro, and Gordon C. Winston. *Paying the Piper: Productivity, Incentives, and Financing in U.S. Higher Education*. Ann Arbor, MI: The University of Michigan Press, 1993.

Middaugh, Michael F. *Understanding Faculty Productivity: Standards and Benchmarks for Colleges and Universities*. San Francisco: Jossey-Bass, 2000.

Middle States Commission on Higher Education. *Student Learning Assessment: Options and Resources*. Philadelphia: Middle States Commission on Higher Education, 2003.

Mintzberg, Henry. *The Rise and Fall of Strategic Planning: Reconceiving Roles for Planning, Plans, Planners*. New York: The Free Press, 1994.

National Association of College and University Business Officers. *Practical Approaches to Rightsizing*. Washington, DC: National Association of College and University Business Officers, 1992.

Nedwek, Brian P., ed. *Doing Academic Planning: Effective Tools for Decision Making*. Ann Arbor, MI: Society for College and University Planning, 1996.

Nichols, James O., et al. *A Practitioner's Handbook for Institutional Effectiveness and Student Outcomes Assessment Implementation*. 3rd ed. New York: Agathon Press, 1995.

Palomba, Catherine A., and Trudy W. Banta. *Assessment Essentials: Planning, Implementing, and Improving Assessment in Higher Education*. San Francisco: Jossey-Bass, 1999.

Peterson, Marvin W., David D. Dill, and Lisa A. Mets, eds. *Planning and Management for a Changing Environment: A Handbook on Redesigning Postsecondary Institutions*. San Francisco: Jossey-Bass, 1997.

Peterson, Marvin W., Lisa A. Mets, Andrea Trice, and David D. Dill, eds. ASHE *Reader on Planning and Institutional Research*. Needham, MA: Pearson Custom Publishing, 1999.

Ratcliff, James L., Edward S. Lubinescu, and Maureen A. Gaffney, eds. *How Accreditation Influences Assessment*. New Directions for Higher Education, no. 113. San Francisco: Jossey-Bass, 2001.

Rose, Rod, ed. *Connecting the Dots...the Essence of Planning*. Ann Arbor, MI: Society for College and University Planning, 2003.

Rowley, Daniel James, Herman D. Lujan, and Michael G. Dolence. *Strategic Change in Colleges and Universities: Planning to Survive and Prosper*. San Francisco: Jossey-Bass, 1997.

Rowley, Daniel James, and Herbert Sherman. *From Strategy to Change: Implementing the Plan in Higher Education*. San Francisco: Jossey-Bass, 2001.

Ruben, Brent D. *Pursuing Excellence in Higher Education: Eight Fundamental Challenges*. San Francisco: Jossey-Bass, 2003.

Schilling, Karen Maitland, and Karl L. Schilling. *Proclaiming and Sustaining Excellence: Assessment as a Faculty Role*. San Francisco: Jossey-Bass, 1998.

Serban, Andreea M., and Jack Friedlander, eds. *Developing and Implementing Assessment of Student Learning Outcomes*. New Directions for Community Colleges, no. 126. San Francisco: Jossey-Bass, Summer 2004.

St. John, Edward P. Prices, *Productivity, and Investment: Assessing Financial Strategies in Higher Education*. San Francisco: Jossey-Bass, 1994.

Suskie, Linda. *Assessing Student Learning: A Common Sense Guide*. Bolton, MA: Anker Publishing, 2004.

Taylor, Barbara E., and William F. Massy. *Strategic Indicators for Higher Education*. Princeton: Peterson's, 1996.

Townsley, Michael K. *The Small College Guide to Financial Health: Beating the Odds*. Washington, DC: National Association of College and University Business Officers, 2002.

Tromp, Sherrie A., and Brent D. Ruben. *Strategic Planning in Higher Education: A Guide for Leaders*. Washington, DC: National Association of College and University Business Officers, 2004.

Waggaman, John S. *Strategies and Consequences: Managing the Costs in Higher Education*. San Francisco: Jossey-Bass, 1992.

Walvoord, Barbara E. *Assessment Clear and Simple: A Practical Guide for Institutions, Departments, and General Education*. San Francisco: Jossey-Bass, 2004.

Walvoord, Barbara E., and Virginia Johnson Anderson. *Effective Grading: A Tool for Learning and Assessment*. San Francisco: Jossey-Bass, 1998.

Acknowledgments

We appreciate the hard work and collaboration of the three former SCUP presidents who authored this book. We should also recognize the support both of the SCUP award-winning University of Delaware, where Middaugh and Hollowell are employed, and of the Middle States Commission on Higher Education, where Sibolski is a senior staffer and Middaugh and Hollowell hold significant positions of volunteer leadership.

In addition, the Society for College and University Planning (SCUP) appreciates the varied but in all instances useful assistance of the following individuals and organizations in the development of the manuscript of this excellent book.

Mark P. Curchak, Dean/Graduate and Professional Studies, Arcadia University

John H. Erickson, Deputy Executive Director, Middle States Commission on Higher Education

Arnold G. Gelfman, Executive Director/Planning, Assessment & Research, Brookdale Community College (NJ), former SCUP board member

John Hammang, Director /Special Projects and Development, American Association of State Colleges and Universities, guest director on SCUP's Board of Directors for 2006–2007

Thomas P. Longin, Executive Editor, Planning for Higher Education (SCUP)

George Mahaffy, Vice President, Academic Leadership and Change, American Association of State Colleges and Universities

Sharon Morioka, editor, former Managing Editor, *Planning for Higher Education*

Melinda G. Spencer, Vice Provost/Administration & Planning, State University of New York at Albany, former SCUP staffer

Joe Szutz, former Assistant Vice Chancellor of Planning, Georgia Board of Regents

L. Carole Wharton, President, L. Carole Wharton, LLC, former SCUP president

Marie E. Zeglin, Senior Vice Provost/Planning & Institutional Effectiveness, Florida International University, Chair of SCUP's Academic Planning Acadmy

Special thanks to George Keller, multiple SCUP award-winner, former editor of Planning for Higher Education, and renowned scholar on strategic planning and higher education. His kind foreword gives SCUP additional confidence that we've produced a valuable resource that will be widely used and accepted throughout the Academy.

The nature of the teamwork in the SCUP office is such that every SCUP staffer had a hand in this book at some point. Those who contributed directly to the product include:

Sunny Beach, SCUP Manager of Media Production

Terry Calhoun, SCUP Director of Media Relations and Publications

Phyllis Grummon, SCUP Director of Education and Planning

Jolene L. Knapp, SCUP Executive Director

About the Authors

David Hollowell is executive vice president and treasurer at the University of Delaware. He was the 1994–95 president of the Society for College and University Planning (SCUP) and the 1997 recipient of SCUP's Distinguished Service Award. He has also served as treasurer of the Board of Trustees of the Middle States Association of Colleges and Schools since 2004.

Michael Middaugh is assistant vice president for institutional research and planning at the University of Delaware. He is the 2005–06 president of the Society for College and University Planning and also served as president of of the Association for Institutional Research in 2000–01. He is a commissioner with the Middle States Commission on Higher Education and national director of the Delaware Study of Instructional Costs and Productivity.

Elizabeth Sibolski is executive associate director of the Middle States Commission on Higher Education and was previously director of university planning and research at the American University in Washington, D.C. She was also the 1998–99 president of the Society for College and University Planning.

CAMBRIDGE UNIVERSITY PRESS
elbourne, Madrid, Cape Town, Singapore, São Paulo, Delhi

Cambridge University Press
of the Americas, New York, NY 10013-2473, USA

www.cambridge.org
n on this title: www.cambridge.org/9780521876322

First published 2008

Printed in the United States of America

alog record for this publication is available from the British Library.

Library of Congress Cataloging in Publication Data

Daniels, Norman, 1942–
Just health : meeting health needs fairly / Norman Daniels.
p. ; cm.
Includes bibliographical references and index.
N 978-0-521-87632-2 (hardback) – ISBN 978-0-521-69998-3 (pbk.)
ical policy – Moral and ethical aspects. 2. Health services accessibility.
t to health care. 4. Equality – Health aspects. 5. Justice (Philosophy)
6. Medical ethics. I. Title.
LM: 1. Health Services Accessibility. 2. Health Policy. 3. Social Justice.
4. World Health. w 76 D186j 2008]
RA394.D27 2008
362.1–dc22   2007011711

ISBN   978-0-521-87632-2 hardback
ISBN   978-0-521-69998-3 paperback

Just Health

In this new book by the award-winning author of *Just Health Care*, Norman Daniels develops a comprehensive theory of justice for health that answers three key questions: What is the special moral importance of health? When are health inequalities unjust? How can we meet health needs fairly when we cannot meet them all? The theory has implications for national and global health policy: Can we meet health needs fairly in aging societies? Or protect health in the workplace while respecting individual liberty? Or meet professional obligations and obligations of justice without conflict? When is health reform or the selection of patients for treatment for HIV or coverage for catastrophic health benefits fair? When is an effort to reduce health disparities or to set priorities in realizing a human right to health fair? What do richer, healthier societies owe poorer, sicker societies? *Just Health: Meeting Health Needs Fairly* explores the many ways that social justice is good for the health of populations in developed and developing countries.

Norman Daniels is Mary B. Saltonstall Professor and Professor of Ethics and Populations Health at Harvard School of Public Health. A member of the Institute of Medicine, a Fellow of the Hastings Center, a Founding Member of the National Academy of Social Insurance and of the International Society for Equity in Health, he has consulted for organizations, commissions, and governments, including the United Nations, WHO, and the President's Commission for the Study of Ethical Problems in Medicine, on issues of justice and health policy. Dr. Daniels is the author of numerous books. He has received fellowships and grants from the National Endowment for the Humanities, the National Science Foundation, and the Robert Wood Johnson Foundation, and he has held a Robert Wood Johnson Investigator's Award as well as a Rockefeller Foundation grant for the international adaptation of the Benchmarks of Fairness for health reform.

For Anne

My constant guide

Cambridge, New York, M

32 Avenue

Informatio

This pub
and to th
n
the

A cat

ISE
1. Med
3. Rigl

[DN

Contents

Acknowledgments

When I was writing my Ph.D. dissertation, my advisor, Hilary Putnam, gave me career-altering advice. He cautioned me that I should do my best in writing my thesis, but that I should understand that knowledge is more a community product than an individual one. He was wisely urging me not to keep my research to myself until I thought it was perfect but to subject it to scrutiny by the philosophical and broader intellectual community, for the critical response to work is as essential to the generation of knowledge as is the care that authors take with their work. I have also learned over my career what people outside philosophy learn early on: that authors' contributions are themselves often a community effort. That is indeed true about this book, for it and the work it reports on would not have been possible without the help of many institutions and many individuals from various disciplines.

My philosophical debts are many. I especially want to acknowledge the many hours of discussion I had in the 1980s and 1990s with John Rawls about justice as fairness and political liberalism and their bearing on health and my approach to it. Joshua Cohen and Dan Brock have been my most generous sounding boards and constructive critics over many years on many of the issues discussed in this book. I also am indebted to others for their help and encouragement on specific issues: Dan Wikler initially encouraged me to address the problems of age and opportunity and gave me constructive criticism about my earlier work in *Just Health Care*; Dan Callahan helped steer me to key issues, including aging and limit setting, over the years; Allan Buchanan forced me to think about the connection of my work to other issues in contemporary work on distributive justice; Ezekial Emanuel broadened my thinking about fair process; Ron Bayer pushed me to reflect on issues of paternalism in occupational health; Frances Kamm's work on various distributive problems has been an inspiration. To acknowledge some of my other philosophical debts, I wish to thank my former Tufts colleagues, Hugo Bedau, Dan Dennett, Erin Kelly, George Smith, and Stephen White, and many others whose comments and conversations have deepened my understanding of relevant normative issues, among them Sudhir Anand, Fabienne Peters, Ole Norheim, Tom Pogge, Matthias Risse, Tim Scanlon, Dennis Thompson, and Amartya Sen.

My greatest debt is owed to the various collaborators who have worked closely with me to develop key ideas that are central to this book. Foremost among them is Jim Sabin, a collaborator for nearly twenty years, who is co-developer of the work on fair process (accountability for reasonableness) that is described in Chapter 4 and that plays a key role in several later chapters. Ichiro Kawachi and Bruce Kennedy worked with me to think through the approach to the social determinants of health and their bearing on health inequalities that is described in Chapter 3. The work of developing the Benchmarks of Fairness in its original form would never have happened without Don Light, whose idea it was, and Ron Caplan. The Benchmarks would never have been adapted for use in developing countries without the key assistance of my collaborators, Jack Bryant and Walter Flores. In addition, many others played important roles in that adaptation: Julio Frenk, who first proposed the adaptation to me, Octavio Gomez-Dantes, Ramon Castano-Yepes, Supasit Pannarunothai, and Kausar Khan. Tim Evans supported the idea with funding from the Rockefeller Foundation. Many others have helped with adaptations in specific countries, especially Peter Ndumbe, T. J. Ngulube, and Yuankun Wang. Sofia Gruskin helped me to develop the approach to priority setting and human rights described in Chapter 12. The work on fair process in Mexico (see Chapter 10) would never have developed without the assistance of Julio Frenk, Octavio Gomez-Dantes, Mercedes Juan, Eduardo Gonzalez-Pier, Cristina Guttierez, and Jason Lakin, among others. I received considerable help on the application of accountability for reasonableness to the WHO 3 by 5 program from Alex Capron and Andreas Reis. I also wish to thank Doug Martin and his crew of researchers at the University of Toronto, who have kept me abreast of work on accountability for reasonableness in Canada and elsewhere. A similar thanks to Ole Norheim at the University of Bergen. Others who have helped me understand relevant issues about the determinants of health or other issues of health policy include Angus Deaton, Chris Ham, Michael Marmot, Marthe Gold, and many of my colleagues at Harvard: Barry Bloom, David Bloom, Tom Bossert, Richard Cash, Nir Eyal, Bill Hsiao, Yuanli Liu, Michael Reich, Joe Newhouse, and Marc Roberts.

I am grateful to many institutions for their support, including Tufts University and Harvard University, for direct and indirect support of my research. Key advances in my thinking on several of the topics were made with the support of a Robert Wood Johnson Special Investigator's Award. I particularly thank the Rockefeller Foundation for multiyear support of the work on adaptation of the Benchmarks of Fairness for developing-country use. The David Rockefeller Center for Latin American Studies and the University of Toronto Global Priority Setting Network have given me support for the work on fair process in Mexico. The work on priority setting has had many sponsors: the Greenwall Foundation, the Robert Wood Johnson Foundation, the National Science Foundation, and the Retirement Research Foundation. My early work on justice and health care was supported by the National Endowment for the Humanities, the National Institutes of Health, and the National Library of Medicine.

I wish to thank as well those who have given me editorial and research assistance with the preparation of this book: Sarah Madsen Hardy, Marin Levy, Danielle Blanch, Linh O, and my wife, Anne. Many students and, more recently, members of the seminar sponsored by the Harvard Program on Ethics and Health have endured earlier versions of this material and have raised questions and provided comments that have gradually improved it. I particularly want to thank Greg Bognar, Eric Cavilierro, Glenn Cohen, Iwao Hirose, Sam Kerstein, Ole Norheim, Diane Paul, and Shlomi Segall for their verbal or written comments on drafts of parts of the manuscript.

I also wish to thank various coauthors, journals, and publishers for permission to draw on some previously published material in drafting some of the chapters in this book:

Daniels, N. 1991. Duty to treat or right to refuse? *Hasting Center Report* 21: 2:36–46.

Daniels, N. 2001. Justice, health and health care. *American Journal of Bioethics* 1: 2:3–15.

Daniels, N. 2003. *Chevron v. Echazabal*: Protection, opportunity, and paternalism. *American Journal of Public Health* 93 4:545–49.

Daniels, N. 2005. Fair process in patient selection for antiretroviral treatment in WHO's goal of "3 by 5." *Lancet* 366: 169–71.

Daniels, N. 2006. Toward ethical review of health system transformations. *American Journal of Public Health* 96: 3:447–51.

Daniels, N. 2006. Equity and population health: Toward a broader bioethics agenda. *Hastings Center Report* 36(4): 22–35.

Daniels, N., Bryant, J., Castano, R. A., Dantes, O.G., Khan, K.S., and, Pannarunothai, S. 2000. Benchmarks of fairness for health care reform: A policy tool for developing countries. *Bulletin of the World Health Organization* 78(6):740–50.

Daniels, N., Flores, W., Ndumbe, P., Pannarunothai, S., Bryant, J., Ngulube, T. J., and Wang Y. 2005. An evidence-based approach to benchmarking the fairness of health sector reform in developing countries. *Bulletin of the World Health Organization* 83: 534–40.

Daniels, N., Kennedy, B., and Kawachi, I. 1999. Why justice is good for our health: The social determinants of health inequalities. *Daedalus* 128(4): 215–51.

Daniels, N., and Sabin, J. 1998. Last-chance therapies and managed care: Pluralism, fair procedures, and legitimacy. *Hastings Center Report* 28(2): 27–41.

Daniels, N., and Sabin, J. 1997. Limits to health care: Fair procedures, democratic deliberation, and the legitimacy problem for insurers. *Philosophy and Public Affairs* 26(4): 303–50.

Introduction

My goal in *Just Health: Meeting Health Needs Fairly* is to present an integrated theory of justice and population health, to address a set of theoretical and real-world challenges to that theory, and to demonstrate that the theory can guide our practice with regard to health both here and abroad. A theory of justice and health must tell us what we owe each other in the protection and promotion of health. To do that, it must explain the moral importance we place on health, it must tell us when differences in health are unjust, and it must guide our thinking about meeting health needs fairly when we cannot meet them all. The answers to these questions are not just theoretical, for they pervasively underlie controversies about health policy and the design of institutions that impact population health. For such a theory to be integrated, the answers to these questions must fit together in a coherent way. Such a theory is validated or tested by examining the way in which it responds to both theoretical and real-world challenges to its central features. It is also tested by the adequacy of the guidance it gives to our practice in promoting and protecting health. My goals are clearly ambitious, but they did not emerge overnight. They accumulated in the course of a long journey that I shall describe.

MY JOURNEY

Just Health: Meeting Health Needs Fairly is the result of an odyssey – physical and intellectual – that began when I published *Just Health Care* over two decades ago. This sequel elaborates in new directions the population view of justice and health that I began to develop in the earlier work, but it is very much the product of my encounters with more practical challenges posed by the wider world of health. Fortunately, my journey was guided by wise collaborators without whom my ideas would never have survived and evolved. I begin my narrative at its starting point, the launch of *Just Health Care*.

1

Since its inception, much of bioethics has focused heavily on important features of the dyadic relationship between doctors and patients or research subjects, or on the potential benefits and risks for those individuals that arise from new technologies, a rich, exotic terrain for ethical exploration. As a political philosopher trained originally in the philosophy of science, I began to write *Just Health Care* with a different, more theoretical and abstract, goal in mind. I thought we could use what I considered to be widespread agreement on how to distribute health care equitably as one way to test which general theories of justice best accounted for that presumed agreement. I quickly discovered that my strategy was naive and that much preliminary work had to be done in order to understand what justice in health means. As a result, *Just Health Care* provided a seminal examination of the social function of health care, broadly construed to include traditional public health and medicine. It focused on social obligations to promote population health and distribute it fairly through its distribution of health care. Like this sequel, it was concerned with more than the benefits that individuals get from public health and medical interventions. Like this sequel, it was concerned with more than the distinctive relationship through which doctors help deliver those medical benefits to individuals who need them.

Yet, the population perspective in *Just Health Care* was partly hidden. Although I had characterized health care broadly to include traditional public health, even devoting two long chapters to occupational health, many of my examples were about medical services. Nor did the title help: "health care" means "medical care" to most people. Not surprisingly, most people then read the book as focused on medical care. The import of focusing on health systems and their impact on populations rather than on individuals was thus blunted. Through my work on priority setting, health system reform, and the social determinants of health, I learned that this limitation of the book was not simply a problem of execution, the result of a focus on the wrong examples. It came from a deeper failure to understand the full dimensions of a population view. My journey taught me that I must seek answers to a broader set of questions.

One central question dominated *Just Health Care*: What is the special moral importance of health and health care? Connecting the answer to that question to prominent work in the general theory of justice was a first step toward articulating a population view since it pointed to the grounds for our social obligations to promote population health and distribute it fairly. Specifically, health is of special moral importance because it contributes to the range of exercisable or effective opportunities open to us. I understand health to mean normal functioning – the absence of significant mental or physical pathology. Maintaining normal functioning through public health and medical interventions thus makes a limited but significant contribution to the range of exercisable opportunities open to people. While opportunity is a good enjoyed by individuals, protecting the space of exercisable opportunities is a societal obligation that creates a public good enjoyed by a population. If we have obligations of social justice to provide equality of opportunity, as in Rawls's robust notion of fair equality of opportunity, then we have social obligations to promote normal functioning and to distribute it equitably in society by designing our institutions properly.

I had high hopes that my answer to the question about the moral importance of health would guide us in resource allocation decisions. I thought that the impact of ill health on opportunity might tell us what we needed to know about the importance of competing health needs. The first stage of my odyssey disabused me of this hope by placing me face-to-face with real-world resource allocation problems.

In the late 1980s, I began to collaborate with James Sabin, a psychiatrist at Harvard Medical School and at the Harvard Community Health Plan. We were interested in how health plans decided to cover one treatment and not another, considering this the tip of the iceberg of resource allocation. The issue of resource allocation – or rationing – had already emerged in U.S. health policy. In the 1980s, Medicare had instituted a prospective payment scheme, diagnosis-related groups (DRGs), which opened a debate about making hospitals and especially physicians act as "gatekeepers" of shared resources. In the late 1980s, Oregon began the process of "rationalizing" its Medicaid coverage decisions, initially using a methodology that ranked treatment–condition pairs by their relative cost-effectiveness. An early lesson of the Oregon process was that the public did not accept a straightforward health-maximizing strategy. At roughly the same time, in the late 1980s, a philosophical literature began to emerge about a set of "unsolved rationing problems," as I later called them (Daniels 1993).[1] These problems were pervasive in health care: How much priority should worse-off cases get? When do minor benefits to large numbers of people outweigh significant benefits to fewer people? When should we give people a fair chance at some lesser benefit rather than invest in the best outcomes? An emerging social science literature later confirmed the view, apparent in the Oregon experience, that many people in various cultures were not straightforward health maximizers (Nord 1999; Dolan et al. 2005).

The collaboration with Jim Sabin took us deep into the decisions about coverage made by managed care organizations and other insurers. We began to understand that reasonable people will disagree about many of the coverage and priority-setting decisions that health insurers in the United States, public agencies in many countries, and even hospitals and local health authorities in many systems have to make. Our adventures in the world of managed care thus led me to see that a population view also required an answer to a distinct question of justice from the one that dominated *Just Health Care*. Now we asked: How can we meet health needs fairly when we

---

[1] Full references for citations in the text are contained in the References.

cannot meet them all? More specifically, given moral disagreement about how to meet health needs, how can priority- or limit-setting decisions come to be accepted as fair and legitimate? Drawing on our initial answer to that question (Daniels and Sabin 2002), *Just Health* integrates our account of a fair process into the rest of my account and develops further its important theoretical and practical implications.

My second adventure brought me face-to-face with yet another central question for population health that I had earlier ignored. In the late 1990s, I became a Robert Wood Johnson Special Investigator. That Fellowship program brought me together with some of the leading American social epidemiologists. Their work on the social determinants of health and of inequalities in health across population subgroups led me to read more widely in the burgeoning field that emerged after I wrote *Just Health Care*. During roughly the same period, U.S. literature began to pay great attention to health inequalities or "disparities" by race. In addition, a growing global literature addressing health inequalities and describing practical efforts to redress some of them became prominent in the same period. After reading this work on health inequalities and their social determinants, I realized that I had pursued the question about the special importance of health – and derivatively of the factors contributing to health – too narrowly. In a collaboration with Bruce Kennedy and Ichiro Kawachi, two researchers at the Harvard School of Public Health, we examined the implications for justice of this literature.

These explorations with Kawachi and Kennedy led me to another key advance that *Just Health* makes over my earlier work, namely, the broader evaluation of all the determinants of health, not just health care or traditional public health. If health has special moral importance because of its impact on opportunity, then these other determinants of health have special importance comparable to that of health care. The broad determinants of health and its distribution in a population include income and wealth, education, political participation, the distributions of rights and powers, and opportunity. These are quite centrally the goods that any general theory of social justice is concerned about. We cannot achieve effective promotion of health in a society as well as its fair distribution without a just distribution of these other goods. Putting together the key results from the social epidemiology literature with Rawls's (1971) principles of justice as fairness, we learn why justice is good for our health and we get a general answer to the question "When is a health inequality unjust?"

The premise of the pun in the title of *Just Health Care* was that I could explain what justice required in health care without talking about all of social justice. I only had to appeal to widespread agreement with the importance of equality of opportunity. In *Just Health,* that premise is undermined, and the pun is replaced with some irony because social justice, broadly construed, promotes population health and distributes it fairly. I nevertheless kept the apparent pun in the title to signal continuity with *Just Health Care*.

The odyssey thus far taught me that my original theory failed to guide practice in significant ways because it had not answered crucial questions. By focusing too narrowly on medical care and traditional public health, rather than on broader determinants of health, the theory failed to give adequate ethical advice about how to reduce unjust health inequalities or even how to identify them adequately. By failing to provide an account of fair process, the theory gave little guidance about how to meet health needs fairly. In the next leg of my journey, my encounters with health system reform, I learned that the integrated population view incorporated in *Just Health* actually provides crucial guidance about the fairness of health reforms.

My experience with health system reform began when I was on the Ethics Working Group of the Clinton Administration Health Care Task Force. We were charged, among other things, with developing "principles" to govern the resulting reform. Before the Task Force convened, I had assembled a set of what I called "design principles" that seemed to be implied by my work on justice and health to that point (see Daniels 1995). The Ethics Working Group, after considerable discussion of the design principles, endorsed a set of principles that Dan Brock and I distilled from our discussion (Brock and Daniels 1994). Although the reform effort soon failed, Don Light approached me about converting my design principles into a matrix for evaluating the reform proposals that had been introduced in the 103rd Congress, and we worked with Ron Caplan to complete that task (Daniels et al. 1996). Our approach combined the ethical framework that had emerged from my thinking about justice and health care with operations research methodology. Measures were developed to assess whether the system was improved or worsened relative to specific goals or criteria – "benchmarks" – of fairness.

In 1998–9, at the urging of Julio Frenk, then head of Fundsalud, a Mexican think tank about health, and more recently the minister of health in Mexico, I collaborated with Jack Bryant and others in Pakistan, Thailand, Mexico, and Colombia to convert the American Benchmarks of Fairness into a generic international version that could be used in a range of developing countries (Daniels, Bryant, Castano, Dantes, Khan, and Pannarunothai, 2000). That version incorporated the broader focus on the social determinants of health with the emphasis on fair process in priority setting. In short, it put the theory in *Just Health* to work monitoring and evaluating health reforms. Since then, with funding from the Rockefeller Foundation, I have worked with Jack Bryant, Walter Flores, and many others to construct local adaptations of the Benchmarks for use in nearly a dozen countries on three continents (Daniels et al. 2005). These many small adventures have led me to conclude that the theory developed in *Just Health* provides practical guidance to those aiming at improved population health, which I take to be an important test of the view.

My odyssey has shaped *Just Health* in structure and content. The following map should help readers find their way. Like Gaul, the book is divided into three parts. Part I lays out the integrated theory. Part II addresses three key challenges to it. Part III puts the theory to use and closes with a final challenge, this time to the reader.

Part I: A Theory of Justice and Health

In Chapter 1, I pose three central questions of justice and suggest how they are related: What is the special moral importance of health? When is a health inequality unjust? How can we meet health needs fairly when we cannot meet them all? I answer each of these questions successively in Chapters 2–4. Chapter 2 builds on my earlier opportunity-based account of the moral importance of health. I find a basis for linking health and opportunity not just in Rawls's (1971) theory of justice as fairness and its later revision (Rawls 1993, 2001), but also in competing accounts of justice (Arneson 1988; G. A. Cohen 1989, 2000; Sen 1992). In Chapter 3, I suggest that the social determinants of health, if governed by an account of justice such as that of Rawls, would significantly reduce observed health inequalities. This suggests that health inequalities are unjust when they result from an unjust distribution of the socially controllable factors affecting population health. In short, social justice is good for our health. In Chapter 4, I argue that we need to supplement an opportunity-based account of the importance of health with an appeal to procedural justice or fair process, since there remain distributive issues that are unresolved by the principle underlying our account of just health. Priority-setting decisions create winners and losers, and moral disagreements about them raise questions of legitimacy. I describe the conditions that must be met in order to achieve accountability for the reasonableness of priority-setting decisions. In Chapter 5, I describe some general implications of the resulting theory for prevention, for a right to health and health care, for disabilities, and for our responsibility regarding health. The answers to our three main questions provide an integrated view of these implications.

Part II: Challenges

Part II responds to three important challenges to the theory. Specifically, the theory must be compatible with the way we think about opportunity over the lifespan, with what we think about the importance of individual liberties, including the liberty to consent to risks, and with what we think about other moral obligations, such as those of physicians to their patients. There are theoretical and real-world aspects of each challenge. In Chapter 6, I consider whether an opportunity-based account of the importance of health can reply to the objection that it would be biased against the elderly, who may be thought to value opportunity less. This challenge is sharpened by the rapidity and magnitude of societal aging globally. Chapter 7 focuses on the conflict between public health approaches to reducing workplace hazards and traditional antipaternalist concerns about letting people consent to risks. In effect, we must consider whether public health is compatible with individual liberty to take risks. These antipaternalist concerns also play a prominent role in more recent disability rights legislation, posing another aspect of the real-world challenge. Chapter 8 explores how well my integrated account of justice fits with claims about the professional obligations of physicians. The challenge comes from the belief, intensified by recent efforts to have physicians play the role of gatekeepers in various countries, that obligations to patients cannot be reconciled with concerns of distributive justice, since these require physicians to act as stewards. The ability of my account of just health to respond to these challenges increases its plausibility.

Part III: Uses

Part III applies my theory to global issues of population health. One key contributor to population health and its fair distribution is the performance of its health system: How well does it pursue the objectives of justice in population health? In Chapter 9, I describe how the theory developed here guided work in developing the Benchmarks of Fairness, a tool for examining how well health sector reforms in low- and middle-income countries work to promote equity, accountability, and efficiency. Chapter 10 describes the relevance of accountability for reasonableness to two quite different problems in developing countries: the difficult task of selecting patients in the global scale-up of HIV/AIDS treatments – an approach endorsed by WHO/UNAIDS (2004), and decision making about the incremental expansion of a catastrophic insurance plan in Mexico. In Chapter 11, I show that efforts to reduce even unjust health inequalities, such as race or gender disparities in health, encounter the unsolved rationing problems noted earlier. The chapter argues that fair process must come to our rescue even when we know that an inequality in health is unjust. Chapter 12 draws on my collaboration with a human rights colleague, Sofia Gruskin, to argue that human rights approaches to health encounter the same priority-setting problems apparent from the perspective of distributive justice and would benefit from the same solution to them.

A Concluding Challenge

The concluding chapter of the book poses a different kind of challenge from those taken up in Part II. It reminds the reader that an account of justice and health is a work in progress, and it poses the challenge of completing that work in a relatively new area of inquiry. From one perspective, the challenge it highlights is a limitation of my theory of just health, namely, that it fails to be specific about international obligations to promote health or reduce international inequalities. I prefer, however, to view the chapter as a challenge to readers or, more accurately, to the global community of which readers are a part. The chapter argues that some international health inequalities are matters for global justice, characterizes a stalemate in the philosophical work on this topic, and proposes a way forward in thinking about our obligations to reduce the inequalities. The challenge to readers is to complete my journey by developing that way forward into a full account of justice and global population health.

By connecting population health to broad questions of social justice, *Just Health* provides a rationale for an expanded focus for bioethics as a field. At the same time, it provides an ethical framework that the many dedicated workers who promote population health here and abroad can use to evaluate the many health policy issues they face. If this framework provides good guidance in thinking about health policy, as I believe it does, the theory will satisfy one important test of normative work. I advance it as a work in progress, not a finished product, a lesson made clear by the developments in my thinking about justice and health over the past couple of decades. I hope others will find ways to improve it so that we can all better understand what justice implies about health.

PART I

A THEORY OF JUSTICE AND HEALTH

1

Three Questions of Justice

A FUNDAMENTAL QUESTION OF JUSTICE

As a matter of justice, what do we owe each other to promote and protect health in a population and to assist people when they are ill or disabled? I shall refer to this question about our social obligations as the "Fundamental Question" of justice for health.

My strategy for answering the Fundamental Question is to substitute for it three more specific "Focal Questions" (Daniels 2001):

1. Is health, and therefore health care and other factors that affect health, of special moral importance? To answer this question, we need to see how meeting health needs is connected with other goals of justice. Answering it may tell us whether we have obligations regarding health and its distribution within a population that do not apply to some other goods.
2. When are health inequalities unjust? To answer this question, we have to understand the factors and social policies that contribute to population health and health inequalities. The answer will help us understand which health inequalities it is most important to address.
3. How can we meet health needs fairly under resource constraints? Since health is not the only important good we pursue, resources are always limited. To answer this question, we must determine the source of our agreements and disagreements about priority setting. This will help guide policy under real-world conditions.

In this chapter, I shall explore each of these Focal Questions further, describe how the answers to them are related to each other, and explain how they fit together to form an answer to the Fundamental Question and thus provide us with a population view of justice and health. The Fundamental Question of justice, in the form of these three Focal Questions, underlies many controversial issues about health policy. My goal in this book is to show that appropriate answers to them offer useful guidance on these policy issues.

Before turning to the Focal Questions, I want to clarify the scope of the Fundamental Question and to warn against some inappropriate starting points in trying to answer it.

Scope of the Fundamental Question

Perhaps the most common way to interpret the Fundamental Question is to view it in terms of medical interventions and services: What kinds of medical treatments should we include in public and private insurance plans? This interpretation is hardly surprising, since most of us believe that modern medicine is what sustains and restores our health. We have generally accepted the idea that modern medicine's magic bullets have made billions of people in the twentieth and twenty-first centuries live the longest and healthiest lives in human history. This focus on medicine and the inspiring myths that surround it is constantly reinforced in our culture by the mass media and by the professional and business interests that are dependent on the medical sector.

The Fundamental Question, however, has a much broader and more radical reach. We can do many other things to and for each other that have a great bearing, arguably more important than that of personal medical services, on the level of health in a population and the distribution of health status in it. For example, as individuals or corporations or communities, we may pollute the water and air, affecting the health of our community and those around it; or, as a society, we may pass and enforce strict environmental protection laws, making the necessary investment to provide all with clean water and air. As a society, we may leave the health and safety of workers in the workplace to the individual or collective bargaining market, or we may enact strict occupational health and safety standards and enforce them. As a community, we may limit access to firearms and require seat belts and airbags in cars, or we may adopt laissez-faire policies. As a society, we may actively educate the public about tobacco, safe sexual practices, and good diet, or we may not. The Fundamental Question asks what traditional public health policies we owe it to each other to pursue. Throughout this book, I will use the term "health care" to include both medical services and public health measures, since both are functionally aimed at individual and population health.

A central theme of this book is that the Fundamental Question reaches beyond health care broadly construed. The dramatic changes in life expectancy and population health status that began over a century ago in many developed countries predate the emergence of even the earliest successes of modern medical technology. Most scientists who have examined the significant rise in life expectancy and health status in much of the twentieth century attribute it to improved nutrition and housing – changes preceding the development of most vaccination programs and coming long before the

.emergence of antibiotics early in World War II. Broad social changes and intersectoral public health measures explain much of the improvement in our longer, healthier lives, more than does modern medicine.

Recent research and literature have focused attention on current health effects of social policies and practices well outside the health sector. As a society, we distribute important goods – such as education, housing, jobs, income, wealth, opportunity, political participation, and a sense of community – very unequally across subgroups that differ by race, ethnicity, gender, or class. These social and economic inequalities then produce health inequalities through complex mechanisms that we are just beginning to understand. We could, if we had the appropriate political understanding and will, limit these inequalities, or at least mitigate their effects through other social policies and practices. The Fundamental Question reaches out broadly to ask about all the "socially controllable factors" – medical care, broader forms of health care, public health measures, and the distribution of non-health-sector goods – that affect the level of population health as well as its distribution. Accordingly, an account of justice for health and health care should tell us how we ought to distribute all of these controllable factors.

The Fundamental Question includes the full range of socially controllable factors that affect health and its distribution. This has immediate implications for the way some philosophers have talked about health and what we owe each other. Rawls (1971), for example, suggests that health (like intelligence) is a "natural good," to be contrasted with social goods, such as health care or education. Understanding the breadth of the social factors that affect levels of population health and its distribution, however, undermines much of the force of this contrast. In whatever sense health is a natural good, its distribution is to a large extent socially determined, as is the aggregate level of health in a population. (The same point can be made about intelligence and cognitive skills more generally.)

A second contrast is even more misleading. Often disease and disability are viewed as natural misfortunes. Illness is just bad luck. But if something is merely unfortunate (as opposed to unfair), then issues of fairness or justice do not arise, or so some people claim.

Again, understanding the breadth of the social factors that affect health and its distribution undermines the view that we are concerned only with cosmic bad luck when we are sick or disabled. This is not to deny that bad luck is often involved. Even where the disadvantage imposed by illness or disability is not the *result* of socially controllable factors, we may still be able to *improve* the situation – by curing the condition or moderating its outcomes and its effects. An account of justice must explain what assistance we owe each other in meeting such needs, even when no one is responsible for making us needy. We should not allow misfortune to beget injustice.[1]

---

[1] Commentators as diverse as the libertarian Englehardt (1981) and the egalitarian Nagel (1997) have appealed to a contrast – or perhaps different contrasts – between what is

Another aspect of the Fundamental Question needs clarification. The question asks about our obligations regarding overall levels of population health, not simply about health inequalities. This may seem surprising, since justice is sometimes described as an account of permissible inequalities. So characterized, it is necessarily concerned with the way health is distributed in a population. For example, a question of justice arises as soon as we observe that the health status of African Americans and some other minorities is worse than that of white non-minority Americans, even when we correct for the effects of differences in education, access to health insurance, and income. Similarly, when we observe that existing race differences in health status in the United States are dwarfed by class differences, further questions of equity – and thus justice – are raised. But it is not so obvious that an account of justice should also be concerned with the overall level of health in a population.[2]

Nevertheless, the Fundamental Question concerns the level of population health. Suppose that we encounter a society in which health status is (approximately) *equally poor* across its population subgroups. Suppose further that there are clear policies that would have improved the level of health in the population had they been implemented; indeed, suppose that they can still be implemented. The simple absence of health inequalities among races, ethnic groups, genders, or classes does not mean that there is no injustice here. After all, social policy has left them all worse off in health than they need be.

An account of justice for health and health care must address this issue. Failing to promote health in a population, that is, failing to promote normal functioning in it, fails to protect the opportunity or capability of people to function as free and equal citizens.[3] Failing to protect that opportunity or capability when we could reasonably do otherwise, I shall argue, is a failure to provide us with what we owe each other. It is unjust.

Where Not to Begin

Faced with concerns about justice – for example, concerns about significant inequalities in health status or health services across races or classes – many people start by invoking the notion of individual or human rights. They assert that a violation of basic rights – a right to health or to health care – is

---

unfortunate and what is unfair. An account of justice must clarify what these contrasts are and what follows from them.

[2] My point is independent of how we measure population health, whether through narrow measures of infant mortality or life expectancy, or through more complex measures that combine length and quality of life, such as healthy life expectancy, disability-adjusted life years, or quality-adjusted life years, thus reflecting the societal burden of disease.

[3] My view is clearly in conflict with Walzer's (1983a, b) claim that a society that ignored health in favor of spiritual goals would be doing nothing unjust.

involved. They believe that the just redesign of health-care institutions or other social structures can be done by appealing to such notions, for people can be galvanized into action when rights they cherish are violated.

Some people who appeal to these rights may assume that health care is more like certain social goods, say certain liberties, to which we assert right claims with clear conviction, than it is like other goods, such as computers or automobiles, to which we do not assert such claims (except as they may derive from property rights in general). Most people who assert a right to health or health care offer no particular theoretical account of its foundations – its grounds or justification – or its limits. They simply hope that if we all acknowledge such a right, we will unite behind the desired reform.

This direct, pragmatic appeal to rights faces significant objections. It does not carry us past our disagreements or uncertainties about the scope and limits of such right claims. It does not tell us what entitlements follow from these right claims. In addition, the pragmatism leaves us well short of determining which beliefs and theories count as an adequate justification for the rights claims. This failure is not just theoretical: It leaves us unable to resolve practical disputes about what these rights imply we owe each other.

My working assumption in this book is that the appeal to a right to health or to health care is not an appropriate starting point for an inquiry into just health or just health care. Rights are not moral fruits that spring up from bare earth, fully ripened, without cultivation. Rather, we may claim a right to health or health care only if it can be harvested from an acceptable general theory of distributive justice or from a more particular theory of justice for health and health care. Such a theory would tell us which kinds of right claims are legitimate. It would also help us specify the scope and limits of justified right claims. My working assumption borders on a philosophical commonplace, shared by many theoretical perspectives, despite the more general practice of the public, which often claims rights wherever strong interests are felt. To answer the difficult questions of what a right to health care or a right to health might include, we need a systematic theory of distributive justice for health-related needs. (I discuss the implications of my view for a right to health and health care in Chapter 5.)

Since we should not begin by appealing to a right to health or health care, should we instead look to general theories of justice that might clarify and justify such rights? Should we not just apply such theories to health and thus answer the Fundamental Question? This suggestion assumes that we can simply apply general theories of justice to the problem of health and health care. Unfortunately, in order to apply general theories to health and the socially controllable factors that affect it, we need to know what kind of a good health is and how its importance to us transfers to the socially controllable factors – medical, public health, and broader social determinants – that protect it. What looks like a natural way from within each theory to make such an application usually presupposes a particular view of the kind of good health or health care is.

One way to see the point is to ask whether health care services, say personal medical services, should be viewed as we view other "commodities" – things we agree to buy and sell in a market – in our society. Should we allow *inequalities* in the access to such services to vary with whatever economic inequalities are permissible according to more general principles of distributive justice? Or is health and therefore health care of special moral importance and not to be assimilated to other commodities, like cars or computers, whose distribution we allow to be governed by market exchanges among economic unequals? Put generally, this is one instance of the Focal Question "Is health or health care special?"

The difficulty can be overcome. The strategy I shall follow in this book is to begin with a more direct analysis of the kind of good that health is, and therefore the kind of importance we should give to health care and the other factors affecting population health and its distribution. Then I shall try to connect this account with more general principles of justice, modifying them if necessary to produce the most plausible fit. Rather than applying these general theories downward to examples of health and health care, I shall try to locate and connect with plausible principles of justice by building on the understanding we can arrive at about the kind of goods that health and health care are (see Chapter 2).

THREE FOCAL QUESTIONS

All inquiry proceeds through questions. Every discipline develops tools and methods for answering the distinctive kinds of questions that define it. To find our way in the thicket of issues about justice and health, as in any area of inquiry, we must ask the right questions.

Each of the three Focal Questions identified earlier addresses a key aspect of the more general Fundamental Question of what we owe each other. If we can explain why societies do and should give special moral importance to meeting health needs, then we may be able to characterize the basis of our obligation to protect health. If we can explain when health inequalities are unjust, then we will have a better idea of what factors affecting population health and its distribution we are obliged to modify through social policy. If we know how to make fair and legitimate priority- and limit-setting decisions about meeting health needs under resource constraints, then we can guide our actions toward more just outcomes under nonideal conditions.

A reader of my earlier work, *Just Health Care*, might wonder why the central question in that book – is health and thus health care of special moral importance? – has now become three questions. Indeed, when I wrote *Just Health Care*, I thought that my answer to the first question sufficed to address the issues raised by the other two. I argued that health care was of special moral importance because protecting health protected opportunity. Since I also thought that health care – broadly construed to include medical services and traditional public health – was the main way to protect health, it seemed trivial to say when a health inequality is unjust. It is unjust when it is the result of unequal access to health care. Since I also thought that the impact on opportunity was the measure of the importance of meeting a health need, I thought I had addressed the question about meeting needs fairly. In short, I thought there was one answer to all key questions about justice and health.

Painful experience taught me that the three questions are distinct. When I learned that a broad range of social determinants of health account for much of the health inequality we see, I saw that the injustice of a health inequality between social groups could not generally be explained solely as the effect of unequal access to medical care or public health protections. When I realized that impact on opportunity could not function as the sole criterion for resource allocation, since there are "opportunity costs" to giving complete priority to those in greatest need and problems about how to aggregate benefits across different people, I saw that the resource-allocation question needed a more general answer. In fact, we could answer any two of the questions without being able to answer the third. It became clear to me that even if I was right about the special moral importance of health, my account failed to guide practice about which health inequalities need to be redressed or about the allocation of resources to meet health needs. In the spirit of learning from my mistakes, I want to motivate each of the three Focal Questions in what follows, liberating the first one as well from any misconceptions about the breadth of the determinants of health.

I do not claim and cannot prove that the Focal Questions are the only way, or even the best way, to organize our inquiry. What I do claim is that each question emerges from a common powerful observation and focuses on a puzzle central to concerns about justice. Each not only concerns a central set of theoretical issues, but also engages with policy issues relevant to them in a fruitful way. I shall first take up each Focal Question briefly to illustrate its centrality and fecundity. I shall then describe briefly the interrelationships of the three questions and suggest how they will fit together to answer the overarching question I began with.

Is Health of Special Moral Importance?

This question was central to my inquiry in *Just Health Care* when I thought health care (broadly understood) was the controllable determinant of population health. It is no less central in *Just Health,* which adds broader social determinants to the socially controllable factors affecting population health and its distribution. The question remains central because the factors that affect health – whatever their scope – derive their moral importance from the moral importance of health.

My focus on the question then and now is driven by the common observation that people who tolerate vast inequalities in wealth and power are often morally outraged when those who are ill cannot get care because they cannot pay for it. People who emphatically reject the general Marxist distributive principle, "From each according to his ability, to each according to his needs," embrace at least the second part of it when applied to health care. Not only individuals but also societies that tolerate – even glorify – significant inequalities in many goods treat health care differently, for they organize public and private cooperative schemes that distribute public health measures and medical services more equitably. Even the United States, the only developed country that fails to provide universal health insurance coverage, proves the rule. It provides universal Medicare coverage to its medically neediest group, the elderly, and publicly funded Medicaid to its very poorest citizens, if not to all in need. The insurance gap in the United States, which grew to 45 million people in 2006 from 33 million when President Bill Clinton attempted to introduce universal coverage in 1993, is widely condemned as unjust. Many poor developing countries have government health care systems that purport to provide universal health insurance coverage, in accord with publicly avowed principles and policy, though in practice they fall well short of doing so.

Are these seemingly schizophrenic attitudes toward social and economic inequality as opposed to health inequality incoherent or do they make moral sense? Why do people ascribe special moral importance to meeting health needs in their social practices? Should they assign it such moral importance? These questions remain central to an inquiry about justice and health even when we understand that the range of factors affecting health is wider than health care.

Many policy controversies relate to disagreements concerning how to answer these questions about the special importance of meeting health needs. The most familiar controversies involve access to medical services. For example, when Medicaid was introduced in the United States in 1965, the claim was made that it should and would avoid a two-class or two-tier medical system in which a distinct set of providers delivers services to the poor. A one-tier system seemed important because of the special importance of health care and because of the morally objectionable nature of inequalities in access to care. The fear of lower-quality health care derived from the widely held belief that "systems for the poor tend to be poor systems." The specific idea was that all physicians would be eligible to accept Medicaid reimbursement.

The outcome, however, proved quite different, in large part because political concessions were made to the medical profession. Physicians are not legally required to participate, and the low reimbursement rates for Medicaid services make these patients unattractive to most physicians. The resulting differentiation between the poor and the middle class – our two-tier reality – means that Medicaid makes an ambiguous statement at best about the special importance of health care.

Even universal coverage systems in other developed countries, which tend to include the poor with the broad middle class, differ about private supplementary insurance schemes that enable the best-off groups to receive faster or slightly better care. Canada and Norway, for example, prohibit the kind of supplementary scheme that the United Kingdom allows, indicating some disagreement about how far to carry the idea of the special importance of medical care. Despite these differences, all share the belief that meeting health care needs has special moral importance.

Private markets for medical insurance raise other questions about the special importance of health care. For example, Americans who buy individual health insurance policies, in contrast to employee-based group insurance policies, must undergo medical underwriting. Their health status and health risk are evaluated by private insurers, which then charge premiums reflecting the purchasers' levels of health risk. Similar underwriting practices are applied to life, property, and liability insurance. In all these cases, private insurers fear that people who are at higher risk and clearly need insurance will be the ones most likely to purchase it (this behavior is called "adverse selection" or "antiselection"). Thus, access to private medical insurance for individuals is not more special than access to other types of insurance, since the people who face the higher risks bear the higher costs. Many view the resulting inequality in access to insurance as unjust. Legislation in the United States in the mid-1990s attempted, with only marginal success, to reduce the exclusion of high-risk individuals from medical insurance.

Views about the special importance of health care affect policies for controlling rising medical costs. One common policy increases cost-sharing by those who use services. For example, Medicare has dramatically raised out-of-pocket expenditures for its patients, shifting the burden of payment to the sickest elderly (the recent Medicare drug benefit is a clumsy attempt to offset part of that problem). Health plans in the United States that once charged only token copayments for pharmacy benefits began, in the mid-1990s, to introduce substantial cost-sharing, either to motivate patients to choose drugs carefully or simply to reduce the proportion of costs borne by employers. Current national and corporate policies emphasize increased cost-sharing through "consumer-driven health plans" such as health savings accounts. These cost-sharing "experiments" (see Chapter 9; also Rosenthal and Daniels 2006) impose significant health risks on vulnerable subgroups. In general, the extensive use of cost-sharing suggests that many legislators, employers, and plan administrators believe that mechanisms for marketing other commodities are also appropriate for health care; that is, they believe that health care may not be as special as some think it should be.

Controversy about the special importance of medical care is not limited to the United States, of course. In the 1990s, many health systems in Europe

experimented with market mechanisms, including efforts to stimulate competition among providers, as a way to improve efficiency. The more emphasis
is placed on such mechanisms, the more we treat health care as a commodity
like any other – possibly undercutting the view that it is of special importance.
Indeed, because the introduction of some market measures threatened the
special moral importance attributed to assuring equity in health care, these
systems had to devise regulations allowing the government to ensure that
equity was not threatened (Saltman 1995). This issue is particularly acute in
many developing countries, where international agencies have encouraged
privatization of many areas of health delivery and increased reliance on out-
of-pocket health expenditures to reclaim health costs. In contrast to many
of the European countries, these developing countries lack the powerful,
reliable state apparatus to limit the tendency of market measures to produce
inequality in access to services (see Chapter 9).

Controversy about the special importance of health care goes beyond the
clinic, the hospital, and medical insurance to include public health policy.
In the United States, for example, early efforts at environmental protection
of workers were threatened by concerns that stringent measures were not
worth the cost to employers or society. Employers sued the Environmental
Protection Agency seeking relief from health and safety standards that were
not "cost-beneficial." Only a crucial decision by the U.S. Supreme Court
in 1978 left intact Congress's intent to protect health to the degree that it
is "technologically feasible" to do so (see Chapter 7). Arguably, this standard reflects, at least in part, the judgment that protecting workers against
workplace health risks is of special moral importance and worth the cost of
developing new technologies to do so. In 2001, the Supreme Court upheld
the authority of the federal government to legislate clean air standards that
are more stringent than those some states would have enacted and more
stringent than a direct calculation of costs and benefits, as preferred by
businesses, might have authorized.

Is health, then, of special moral importance? What gives it that importance? Does that importance extend to the socially controllable factors that
promote health?

Chapter 2 builds on the answer I gave to these questions in *Just Health
Care*.[4] We keep people functioning normally by meeting their health needs,
not just by providing health care but also by properly distributing the socially

---

[4] To support the view that health care is of special moral importance, some offer what I called
the "Argument from Function" in *Just Health Care*. (a) The function of medical services is to
meet medical needs. (b) The sole rational basis for distributing a good that meets certain
needs is in proportion to those needs. (c) Therefore, the sole rational basis for distributing
medical services is to meet medical needs. (d) Health status should determine access to
medical needs.

This argument will not do as it stands. The *function* of lawn mowers is to meet lawn-mowing
needs. No one insists, as a result, that willingness to pay for lawn mowers is the wrong basis
for distributing them and that those who cannot afford them should be subsidized. Clearly,

controllable factors that affect population health. The loss of function associated with disease and disability reduces the range of opportunities open to us compared to what it would be were we healthy or fully functional. By keeping people functioning normally, we protect their range of opportunities. If we have a social obligation to protect opportunity in this way, then we have a general framework for thinking about justice and health. One general theory of justice that justifies a principle protecting opportunity is Rawls's theory of justice as fairness (Rawls 1971, 2001). My claim about the relationship between health and opportunity thus provides a way of extending Rawls's theory to address the inequalities created by disease and disability, a key issue that Rawls had deliberately avoided. The extension vastly increases the power of his theory and its ability to respond to some critics. Other work on distributive justice that was developed after Rawls's initial work, and in part in response to it, also provides some support for the connection between health and opportunity and for the claim that we have some obligations of justice to protect opportunity.

In short, health is of special moral importance because it contributes to the range of opportunities open to us. Therefore, the socially controllable factors that promote health – medical services, traditional public health, and the distribution of the broader social determinants of health – derive special importance from their contribution to protecting opportunities. My move from *Just Health Care* to *Just Health* retains the core explanation of the connection between health and opportunity, but it expands the factors that derive importance from that connection because of their impact on population health and its distribution.

When Are Health Inequalities Unjust?

Even if we know that health is of special moral importance because of its impact on opportunity, and even if we have an obligation to protect equality of opportunity, we do not know when health inequalities across social groups are unjust. If we think health care is the only way society has of protecting health, then, as I noted earlier, we might (mistakenly) infer that health inequalities are unjust when access to health care is unequal. The importance of this second Focal Question rests on understanding the many socially controllable factors that affect health inequalities. Answering the question will help us understand the breadth of what justice requires us to do to protect population health and its fair distribution.

The second Focal Question emerges from the common observation that health inequalities across social groups – by race or ethnic group, class, or

if the Argument from Function has any merit, it is only with regard to a special class of needs and things that function to meet them. We are back to a specific version of our first Focal Question, "Is health care special?"

gender – occur in all societies. In every society, for example, we find a "social gradient" of health. If we graph life expectancy, a crude measure of health, or healthy life expectancy, a somewhat more precise measure of health, against socioeconomic status, we find that the richer (and, in the United States, the whiter) people are, the healthier and longer their lives. Different countries will have steeper or flatter gradients, depending on many facts about their distribution of other goods, such as education, income, wealth, housing, and access to health care. In the United States, when we control for inequalities in income, education, and insurance coverage, we still find significant racial inequalities in life expectancy and morbidity. Similar inequalities among racial and ethnic groups can be found in many countries. What is more, the class, race, and gender inequalities found in many countries cannot be explained simply by the presence or absence of poverty and deprivation; they persist well up the socioeconomic ladder and are significantly affected by bias associated with cultural and religious practices.

These inequalities persist even in developed countries that invest heavily in public health and assure universal coverage for medical services. Indeed, the presence of universal-coverage health systems has only a modest effect on health gradients, which are more sensitive to the distributions of other goods. Some of these health inequalities we may not know how to avoid or modify. Others, however, are clearly related to social policies that distribute many other important goods, such as education, income and wealth, and effective political participation. We may have various goals that lead to these social policies, and some of them may be required by other considerations of justice.

Are all of these commonly observed health inequalities unjust? Should we view some of them as acceptable trade-offs against other things we also value highly in society? Although our answer to the first Focal Question suggests that health and health care are of special moral importance because of their effects on opportunity, opportunity is not the only thing we value. However important, it is not the only good of special moral importance, even from the perspective of justice. In short, the second Focal Question is important because it reminds us that what justice requires in policy that affects health and the acceptability of health inequalities must be compatible with what justice requires in the distribution of a broad range of social goods. The fact that health is not simply the product of health care means that we cannot easily isolate health from broader social justice (as I thought we could in *Just Health Care*).

The second Focal Question underlies many important policy controversies. Often it is claimed that we must accept some, perhaps a great deal of, inequality in order to stimulate economic development in developing countries or more rapid growth in any country. If, to promote development or growth, we must accept significant inequalities, then we may be inducing health inequalities. There is much controversy in developing countries about the consequences of different approaches to acceptable socioeconomic inequalities. For example, some people claim that we can reduce poverty most rapidly by accepting significant inequalities; as a result, countries may reduce health inequalities more than they would if they accepted a slower rate of growth. Others insist that policies improve population health more if they aim directly at producing a more equal distribution of health, even if this means a slower rate of growth. In developed countries, there are similar controversies about the consequences of different degrees of economic inequality. Some argue that jobs are created more quickly if we allow greater economic inequality and provide a narrower social safety net; others say that a broader social safety net and the redistribution it involves make the effect of unemployment more bearable and reduce health inequalities more. These controversies, I suggest, are not just about *empirical* uncertainty. They also reflect underlying moral disagreements about what kinds of inequality, and what trade-offs among them, are morally acceptable or fair.

Chapter 3 offers an approach to answering the second Focal Question. To answer it, we must not only understand the socially controllable factors that affect population health and its distribution, but also have an account of when the distribution of these factors is fair or just. As I noted, for example, it is not enough simply to say that poverty is unjust and whatever health inequality follows from dire poverty is therefore unjust. Instead, we must have an account of when income inequalities are fair or just – despite or including their effects on health.

My approach to this question is based on a striking observation: The general principles of justice that Rawls argues for in his theory of justice as fairness capture the key social determinants of health, especially if one includes, as I do, health care in the institutions that protect opportunity. If Rawls's principles constitute a fair distribution of these socially controllable factors affecting health, then we may have made some headway in deciding which health inequalities are unjust. Using this approach, one might say that the inequalities in health that remain after a fair distribution of other goods should count as acceptable or fair inequalities. Others, however, may read the priority Rawls ascribes to opportunity as requiring a further reduction in health inequalities. Despite this controversy about remaining health inequalities, the appeal to Rawls to illustrate what a fair distribution of determinants of health might look like is a distinct advance over the simpler extension of his theory provided by my answer to the first Focal Question.

In effect, my answer to the second Focal Question suggests that justice as fairness is good for our health. It arguably leads to a fair distribution of population health, and it does so in a way that social justice in general endorses. This answer is particularly startling since Rawls simplified the development of his theory by postulating that all people function normally over a normal lifespan, barring the prospect of disease and disability from his social contract. What is startling is that a theory that develops an account of social and political well-being turns out to generalize into a theory that provides for our physical and mental health as well. The answer is, however, only a partial answer, and I shall examine its adequacy.

How Can We Meet Health Needs Fairly under Resource Limits?

Even if we have acceptable answers to the first two Focal Questions, we will face further challenges presented by the third: How can we meet health needs fairly under reasonable resource limits? Suppose that we agree about how much moral importance we should attribute to meeting health needs, because we understand the connection between health and opportunity. Suppose that we also agree about which health inequalities we find unjust, and suppose that we even agree on what we consider reasonable resource limits on efforts to meet health needs. Unfortunately, all this agreement still does not tell us how to meet conflicting health care needs fairly when we cannot meet them all. We observe that all societies face this problem, even when they have a social consensus on the importance of health and a good grasp of the measures that may affect the distribution of population health. Although an answer to the third Focal Question is not provided by answers to the other two Focal Questions, the answer must still be compatible with these other answers.

The problem raised by the third Focal Question arises because we lack a consensus on principles for resolving conflicting claims on resources for meeting health needs.[5] For example, Rawls's principle assuring fair equality of opportunity as a basis for the social obligation to promote health is too general and indeterminate to help us make specific resource-allocation decisions. It might incline us to favor giving greater priority to those whose health is worse off, since their opportunities are more seriously reduced. But few would accept giving complete priority to those who are worst off, especially if that meant not meeting the health needs of others who have significant, but less serious, illnesses. Different people would make these trade-offs in different ways. We lack a principled account of how they should be made.

Other familiar areas of reasonable moral disagreement are revealed when a public or private insurer denies coverage for a "last-chance" therapy that is not fully proven but that offers an individual her only hope. Reasonable people may disagree about how much weight to give to stewardship of scarce resources and how much to compassionate use of these resources for specific individuals. Again, we lack agreement on principles that can resolve this dispute.

---

[5] Actually, the problem is general (Daniels 1993) and arises for claims about other needs as well, but I focus here on health needs.

Any decision we make about how to use resources to meet health needs can create winners and losers. Yet, we lack a consensus on principles for resolving disputes among these winners and losers. We have reasonable moral disagreement about how to treat people fairly. Perhaps we can eventually arrive at philosophical analyses of these issues that produce wide acceptance of appropriate principles, and we should invest in such work, but in the real world, resources must be allocated in real time in a way that is perceived to be legitimate and fair.

Chapter 4, drawing on my work with Jim Sabin (Daniels and Sabin 2002), proposes that we rely on a fair deliberative process to reduce disagreements about resource allocation. This is an appeal to procedural justice: The outcomes of fair procedures should count as fair when we cannot agree on principles for resolving the disputes. The specific conditions such a process should satisfy – publicity of rationales, a search for relevant reasons that are properly vetted by those affected by the decision, opportunity for revising decisions in light of new evidence and arguments, and assurance that these conditions are uniformly enforced – make decision makers accountable for the reasonableness of their decisions. They provide the conditions for the legitimacy of controversial decisions. At the same time, this fair process should be limited by the considerations of justice that emerge from our answers to the first and second Focal Questions. A complete account of just health and just health care must appeal both to principles and to process, and the two components must cohere appropriately.

Like the first two Focal Questions, the third one underlies policy controversy in addition to posing a theoretical puzzle. For example, the policy problem of access to health care breaks down into two questions: Who has access? To what do they have access? The latter question has become increasingly central to policy discussions in the United States and elsewhere. Since medical services today deliver vastly more expensive, varied, and effective products than they did years ago, it has become crucial to limit care. At whatever level of funding a society establishes as reasonable for it – from 6 percent in the United Kingdom to over 14 percent in the United States, it is still not possible to meet all competing health needs. Limits must be set.

Controversy focuses on what limits are fair and how they can be set in a fair way. One volatile form of this controversy is the frequent protest against denials of care, especially when people are desperately ill and all proven medical remedies have failed. In Cambridge, England, great media controversy surrounded the Cambridge Health Authority's denial of an experimental treatment to Child B (Ham and Pickard 1998). In Boston, Massachusetts, similar media controversy focused on Medicaid denial of an unproven therapy for a dying child. In both cases, private charitable donations were used to obtain the (unsuccessful) treatments. In the early 1990s in the United States, litigation and legislation made bone marrow transplants the standard of care for treating advanced breast cancer, delaying the results of clinical trials that later showed that these treatments actually reduced life expectancy.

It is not just last-chance therapies that are the focus of limit setting. Most cost reduction in the United States throughout the 1980s resulted from limits on hospital stays for which insurers (especially Medicare) would reimburse hospitals. (By squeezing hard on length of hospital stay, payers produced a bulge elsewhere in the balloon of medical costs, since new technologies were encouraged that led to the costly delivery at home of services previously available only in hospitals.) Since the mid-1990s, drug costs in the United States (and elsewhere) have been rising at a rate of over 10 percent per year, making them the fastest-growing part of the health care budget. The private for-profit companies that manage the drug benefits for most insured Americans have adopted various strategies for limit setting. Yet, the establishment of limited formularies and various types of copayment has produced much discontent among patients and physicians. It has also produced much confusion in the implementation of the Medicare Part D drug benefit.

During the 1990s in the United States, physician reimbursements were restructured from the common fee-for-service arrangements of previous decades to various types of income withholding and capitatiou. These new arrangements give physicians incentives to reduce utilization, but they also increase distrust. Patients fear that they will be undertreated by physicians who try to increase earnings. (Apparently, the fear of undertreatment is greater than the fear of overtreatment, which was the clear risk of fee-for-service incentives.)

Supplementing a principled account of justice and health with an appeal to fair process where principles do not resolve disputes is a strategy that many philosophers find problematic. Many resist the idea that philosophical investigation cannot produce a consensus on the right view; there is considerable distrust of a fair process that is open to abuse and misuse and can end up "merely political" in the worst sense. Nevertheless, the approach I describe has wide appeal in practical settings where the challenge of reasonable disagreement must be met.

A POPULATION VIEW OF JUSTICE AND HEALTH

Answers to the three Focal Questions cohere to provide an answer to the Fundamental Question about what we owe each other in promoting our health and assisting each other when we face illness or disability. Together the three answers offer a population view of justice and health. Chapters 2–4 develop these answers in greater detail, and Chapter 5 describes some of their central implications. Before embarking on those more detailed tasks, I want to make sure that the big picture remains clear. I need to say more about how the answers fit together to form an integrated population view.

My answer to the first Focal Question shows that the special moral importance of health derives from its impact on our opportunities. Thus, it explains why protecting health is a social obligation, not simply one on individuals with particular roles, such as physicians. As members of a society seeking fair terms of cooperation to protect each other's health, we owe it to each other to design institutions that do that and create a collective space to protect opportunity in this way. This claim about the importance of protecting opportunity is supported by many general theories of justice (though obviously not all).

My answer to the second Focal Question is that a health inequality is unjust when it derives from an unjust distribution of the socially controllable factors affecting population health and its distribution. I illustrated what is meant by a just distribution of those determinants of health by noting how Rawls's principles of justice as fairness would distribute them. This answer explains why and how all groups are included in the collective obligation to promote health, why none should be left out or neglected, and how we can tell which groups are being shortchanged. To answer this Focal Question, we must identify the sources of health inequality in populations and learn how to correct them.

Despite the principled account that emerges from these first two answers, a problem remains. The principles are too indeterminate to tell us how to resolve disputes among those with legitimate claims on resources for meeting health needs. Reasonable people disagree about how those claims should be addressed, despite the general guidance provided by the answers to the first two Focal Questions. My answer to the third Focal Question shows that we must supplement guidance from general principles with a fair deliberative process. Only in this way can the choices that unavoidably create winners and losers among reasonable claimants on assistance be viewed as legitimate.

In short, my answers to the three Focal Questions address the central issues involved in justice and population health: We understand the basis on which we owe people assistance in protecting health. We can tell when some people or groups are being treated less fairly than others, and we see more clearly what we should do about it. We understand how to arrive at fair and legitimate decisions about competing health needs when we cannot meet them all.

These answers limit each other in important ways. The appeal to fair process is intended to resolve disputes about how best to protect the opportunities of groups with competing claims on health resources. Relying on fair process to set limits and priorities for resource allocation does not replace broader obligations of justice to protect opportunity and distribute other goods fairly; rather, it is limited by those obligations. It is a way to produce agreement about what those obligations mean in a world of competing claims. Similarly, answers to the first two Focal Questions limit each other.

Thus, the connection between health and opportunity has a bearing on when health inequalities between groups are unjust: Health inequalities that are unjust must have something to do with unjustifiable inequalities in the resulting opportunities for people. Conversely, these inequalities in opportunity become unjustifiable, depending on the rationale for the distribution of the determinants of health.

Integrating these answers thus gives us a population view of just health. Together they tell us how a society should organize itself to address its health needs equitably. This focus on equity must nevertheless be compatible with other concerns of social justice, which I pursue in Part II. Moreover, a population view of health must be global, some aspects of which I consider in Part III.

2

What Is the Special Moral Importance of Health?

People in many societies consider it outrageous if the social and economic inequalities they generally accept interfere with people's ability to get what they need to prevent or cure illness. They convert belief into action by designing and financing health-care institutions that deliver public health and medical services more equitably than many other goods. What is so special about meeting health-care needs? Can we justify these beliefs and practices?

Not surprisingly, the answers to these questions depend on explaining the special moral importance of health itself, at least from the point of view of justice. Once we can explain why health is of special moral importance, we can explain why special importance is given to meeting health-care needs equitably. That was the strategy of my central argument over two decades ago in *Just Health Care*: (1) Since health care promotes health (or normal functioning), and since health contributes to protecting opportunity, then health care protects opportunity. (2) If justice requires society to protect opportunity, then justice gives special importance to health care. Instead of showing directly that justice requires protecting opportunity, however, I borrowed support for that claim from Rawls's theory of justice as fairness and its robust principle assuring fair equality of opportunity. In effect, I could then replace (2) with (3) Since Rawls's justice as fairness requires protecting opportunity, then at least one prominent theory of justice gives special importance to health care. My borrowing in this way from Rawls's theory actually increases its power. The connection that I established then between health and opportunity shows how to extend Rawls's theory so that it can accommodate the facts about disease and disability that it had (deliberately) ignored.

This chapter extends my earlier strategy in two ways. First, I generalize the answer about the special moral importance of health in order to explain why health needs generally, and not just health care, are so important. Health care is but one of many socially controllable factors that affect population health and its distribution. It is but one of a broader set of health needs. Second, to support my claim that justice obliges us to protect opportunity, I discuss recent theories that compete with Rawls's view of distributive justice. Despite their differences with Rawls, these accounts of justice emphasize the importance of protecting opportunity. If I am right that meeting health needs protects opportunity, these views also support my claim that health is of special moral importance because it contributes to protecting opportunity.

These extensions lead to this revised central argument: (1′) Since meeting health needs promotes health (or normal functioning), and since health helps to protect opportunity, then meeting health needs protects opportunity. (2′) Since Rawls's justice as fairness requires protecting opportunity, as do other important approaches to distributive justice, then several recent accounts of justice give special importance to meeting health needs.

Establishing (1′) is largely a conceptual and explanatory task. It requires us to clarify the concepts of needs and health, since both are controversial. Explaining the importance of meeting health needs then rests on people's interest in protecting normal functioning and thus their range of opportunities. We should expect two things from a theory of health needs that fits with this strategy. First, it should show how these needs are connected to other central notions, such as opportunity, in an acceptable theory of justice, thus clarifying how health care is special.[1] Second, it should provide a basis for distinguishing the more from the less important kinds of things meeting health needs does for us, at least intuitively and roughly, even if it cannot resolve reasonable disagreements about resource allocation (as noted in Chapter 1 and elaborated in Chapter 4). The first main section of this chapter addresses these tasks.

To establish (2′), I borrow justification for thinking that we are required to protect opportunity from several lines of recent work in the general theory of justice. In the second main section of this chapter, I show how to integrate our account of health needs with Rawls's theory, extending his theory in ways he embraced in his later work. In the third main section of this chapter, I show that even some of Rawls's critics agree that we have an obligation to protect the range of our exercisable opportunities. The revised central argument thus answers the first Focal Question, "What is the special moral importance of health?"

---

[1] I am not giving an anthropological explanation that says that people believe health protects opportunity and they value opportunity. If asked, people may say that they think health care is important for many reasons, including the fact that it saves lives or reduces suffering. My explanation reflects people's real interests and coheres well with the justification for thinking that meeting health needs is morally important, namely, that we have an obligation to protect opportunity and that protecting health protects opportunity.